THE STORY OF NORTHAMPTON

THE STORY OF NORTHAMPTON

BY

A. P. White, M.A., Oxon.

Republished by S. R. Publishers, Ltd., 1970.

First Published by W. Mark and Co., Ltd., Northampton

1914.

ISBN 0 85409 573 X

Reproduced and Printed in Great Britain by
Redwood Press Limited, Trowbridge and London.

THE OLD CASTLE OF NORTHAMPTON. (FROM THE NORTH-WEST).
Reproduced from The Rev. R. M. SERJEANTSON's "Castle of Northampton," by permission of the Author, and the Northants. Natural History Society.

THE STORY OF NORTHAMPTON.

BY

A. P. WHITE, M.A., Oxon.

SENIOR HISTORY MASTER, NORTHAMPTON SCHOOL.

NORTHAMPTON:

W. MARK AND CO., LTD., 27 THE DRAPERY.

—

1914.

PRINTED BY
W. MARK AND CO., LTD., 27 THE DRAPERY,
NORTHAMPTON.

PREFACE.

MY aim in writing this little book has been to provide a short, accurate, and readable history of Northampton, from the earliest times until the recent visit of King George V. Although the book is primarily designed for use in schools, it is hoped that it will also give pleasure to those of the general public who take an interest in the past history of the town.

I desire to express my gratitude to the Rev. R. M. Serjeantson for the great help that he has given me, while I have been writing this history. Not only am I indebted to him for many valuable suggestions and corrections, but also it is largely due to his previous research work that much of the material used in this book has been brought to light.

Mr. T. J. George, the well-known local authority on the history of primitive man, has given me much help with the earlier part of the book.

Mr. S. S. Campion has very kindly read the manuscript through, and has offered numerous suggestions of the greatest possible value.

I have also to thank Mr. E. Reynolds, Mr. S. S. Sopwith, and Mr. F. C. M. Richards, all of the Northampton School, for their help in revising the text of this book. Miss F. M. White, of the Godolphin School, Salisbury, has assisted me throughout, more especially in the correction of the printer's proofs. Miss White has also undertaken to arrange the final details of publication, to which I have been unable to give much attention.

The plates in this book have been reproduced from blocks in the possession of Rev. R. M. Serjeantson, Mr. C. A. Markham, and from those lent by the Editor of the *Independent*, I wish to tender my sincere thanks to these gentlemen for their kind permission to use the blocks.

CONTENTS.

CHAPTER I.

BEFORE THE BRITONS CAME.

ALMOST every boy who lives in Northampton has, at one time or another, climbed to the top of the hill upon which the enclosure known as Danes' Camp is situated, and then has paused to gaze back at the town. There, beneath him, it lies; a mighty mass of buildings spread out from the Nene to the distant horizon. Perhaps a glow of pride comes to him as his eye sweeps over the wide expanse of roofs, the towers and spires of the many churches, and the great factories and tall chimneys that tell of a prosperous and flourishing industrial town; he says to himself, in the words of St. Paul, " I am a citizen of no mean city."

As he looks around him he sees that all is quiet on the hill; probably not another human being is in sight in the immediate neighbourhood of the camp. Far away below, he knows that the Northampton streets are full of life, movement, and stir, as people pass hither and thither about their daily work, but here is solitude and stillness.

It seems hard to realise that some 2,000 years ago these conditions were reversed. Here, on Hunsbury Hill, was the centre of life and activity, gathered around the old British *dun*, or hill-fort, much of which is still left. Below, where the town now lies, there was not a house standing, nothing save a wild and trackless forest sloping down to the marshes that fringed the river. Little did the Britons, whose stronghold overlooked the site occupied by our town to-day, imagine the changes that time would bring.

But, to trace the history of man in this district, it is necessary to go back far beyond the Britons. They were by no means the earliest race to inhabit the country. It is not known exactly how long ago it was when the first human beings trod upon the slopes that lead down to the Nene, but undoubtedly the time must be measured in thousands of years.

Life must have been hard for the earliest men that lived here, and only the strongest and most cunning among them can have survived long enough to leave any descendants. They were, in all probability, small, stunted, hairy creatures, and from the few, the very few, remains of their skulls that have been found in various parts of the world, it is thought that their heads were less round than ours, and longer from front to back. They went about either entirely without clothes, or roughly clad in the skins of animals; they could not till the ground, they knew nothing of metals, and they did not understand the use of fire. The only weapons they possessed were sharpened pieces of flint, which they held in their hands. For this reason they are generally called Palæolithic men. The word Palæolithic is of Greek origin and means "old stone"

There does not seem to have been any regular settlement of these Palæolithic men near the site of modern Northampton, but there are sufficient relics of them left to afford evidence of their presence here at some past time A visit to the Town Museum will enable the reader to see some of the flint weapons that primitive man used in his unending fight against the animals upon whose flesh he depended for food There, too, may be seen the curved tusks and huge teeth of the gigantic mammoth, and other remains that tell us of the strange beasts that once lived here. Most of these relics have been found in the gravel drifts above the Nene, which then ran at a far higher level than that of its present course.

In Northamptonshire there are no traces left of the "cave-men," as the later Palæolithic men are called to distinguish them from the earlier "drift men," whose implements are found in the river drifts. The next race, therefore, to be noticed is that of the Neolithic, or "new stone" men. These men were a far superior type to the earlier inhabitants of the land, whom they perhaps displaced by force. They were an oval-faced short, dark-haired people, with sallow skins and black, flashing eyes. Men like this are often found among the modern Welsh, who are in part descended from the Neolithic men, but the people to whom these early men are most akin are the Basques, a mountain race who still inhabit the Pyrenees. For this reason the Neolithic men are often called Iberians, because Iberia is an old name for Spain.

As they did not come to England until after the separation of this island from the continent, the Neolithic men must have been able to construct boats of some kind. Like the Palæolithic men, they did not use metal at all, but in many other respects they were greatly in advance of the earlier race. They made fires and knew how to plough the ground and to sow seeds; they kept herds of cattle; they lived in villages, unlike the Palæolithic men, who had slept in the open or in caves.

One of their villages was situated quite near to our town, between the Nene and Duston. Here they hewed down the trees with their stone axes and made a clearing, in which their settlement was built. No less than 20,000 of their flints have been found near the spot, so they must have lived there for many years.

Neolithic implements are very different from the roughly sharpened hand-flints of the Palæolithic men. These later settlers used axes, axes with beautifully polished stone blades tied on to the top of a stout wooden handle. To slay at a distance, they had bows and arrows, the latter being tipped with a sharply pointed flint. They had also keen-edged flints for scraping off the skins of the animals that they had killed. When the Northampton School in the Billing Road was being built a few years ago, the workmen who were digging the foundations of the building brought to light one of these "scrapers." The scraper lay embedded in the earth, in much the same position as it was when the hunter, who once owned it, lost it there thousands of years ago.

The wooden handles of the Neolithic axes and the shafts of the arrows have long since crumbled away to dust, but flint is a lasting substance, so the axe-blades and arrow-heads are to be seen in the Museum, little changed by time. A careful examination of these implements will show that the skill and patience necessary to produce such work must have been truly marvellous.

Thus, century after century, these Neolithic men lived and died in the clearing by the river side. Perhaps they had wars with other tribes, wars which seemed very important to them, but of which no record has come down to us. On the whole, however, Neolithic man seems to have been of a fairly peaceful disposition, content to till the land and to follow the chase, without quarrelling with his neighbours.

Then, one day, rumours must have reached the village of a coming of a strange people from the sea Fair, tall, round-headed men these were, with wonderful weapons made of some unknown substance, such as had never been seen before in the land. They were marching in the direction of the village and subduing all opposition by means of their superior arms. In time, these strange men reached the Nene Valley, and the land passed into their hands. These newcomers, who are generally spoken of as the Goidels, belonged to the great Celtic race. They were the first people in this island to understand the use of metals, and they fought with weapons made of bronze.

For many years the Goidels held the land they had won, but at last they were dispossessed in their turn by a fresh swarm of invaders from the continent. These were another branch of the Celtic race, and they were called the Britons. They defeated the Goidels for the same reason that the Goidels defeated the Neolithic men—because they had better weapons. The Britons knew how to smelt iron and made their swords and spear-heads of that metal. The Goidels, with their soft bronze weapons, had but little chance against the better armed invaders, and so again the land changed hands.

Thus we have seen that the Neolithic men conquered the Palæolithic men, the Goidels conquered the Neolithic men, and the Britons conquered the Goidels. These Britons, who gave our island the name by which it is still sometimes known, constructed the enclosure on Hunsbury Hill that is generally called Danes' Camp.

CHAPTER II.

THE DUN ON HUNSBURY HILL.

AFTER reading in the previous chapter how this country was overrun by one invading race after another, each conquering the race that had preceded it, the question that at once occurs to everyone is, "What happened to the vanquished people in each case?"

This question is a very hard one to answer accurately, and it is very easy to misunderstand the answer unless it is carefully explained. It is generally said that the Palæolithic men fled overseas to the north, and that the Eskimos are their direct descendants, that the Neolithic men were driven into Wales, Ireland, and the extreme north of Scotland, and that the descendants of the Goidels are to be found in the Isle of Man, in the Scottish Highlands, and in Ireland.

This is undoubtedly true, in a sense, except perhaps as regards Palæolithic man, of whom nothing certain is known. What must be realised is that the same thing did not happen everywhere. No doubt some of the inhabitants fled before the invaders to the mountainous parts of the country, or across the sea. Many, of course, were slain in battle or massacred after the fight was over. Still, we can be sure that very often whole tribes, terrified by the fate of those who resisted, yielded at once to the conquerors and were allowed to live on, under the rule of the victorious race, in the villages that they had occupied before. Even when resistance was offered, many prisoners would be taken. Their fate would depend largely upon the character of the chief of the invading force that conquered that particular district, but, apart from any question of mercy, slaves were of value, and this fact alone must have saved the lives of many captives.

So it need not be imagined that all the old inhabitants were driven out or slain whenever the land was conquered by an invading race. We may think of the Britons who built Danes' Camp as being in part descended from earlier races who had yielded to their conquerors, and in time had intermarried with them. Indeed, the Britons do not seem to have entirely abandoned the Neolithic settlement near Duston. They saw, however, that the clearing by the river was not very favourably situated for defence against fresh attacks, and perhaps it was for this reason that they built the *dun*, or hill-fort, that stands on Hunsbury Hill.

It is hard to say how this place gained the name of Danes' Camp, as there is no reason whatever for connecting it with the Danes. A gentleman writing on this subject about 200 years ago said, "I attribute it to the Danes the rather because I see not to whom else it should belong." This is a very good example of the guesswork upon which many of the conclusions of the 18th century historical writers were based. We have now a more certain foundation upon which to rest our opinions, for some years ago the ground there was thoroughly dug up in order to extract the iron-stone, and in the course of this excavation an enormous number of relics were discovered, relics which give us a fairly accurate idea of the date at which the dun was occupied.

Hitherto we have not been able to make any estimate as to when the different races that we have mentioned lived in this district. We have seen that there was a Stone Age, a Bronze Age, and an Iron Age, but it is impossible to say how long each period lasted. Moreover, bronze did not at once displace stone, nor did iron at once displace bronze. A modern illustration will perhaps show more clearly what is meant by this statement. We are now living in the age of electricity, but electric light had not yet displaced gas in every house, while in country districts gas has not even yet displaced the oil lamp. Similarly in primitive times iron, bronze, and stone were used side by side, just as electricity, gas, and oil are used to-day.

Still, we can judge from the articles found at Hunsbury Hill that the *dun* was occupied by people who were thoroughly acquainted with the use of iron. This makes us sure that it was inhabited during the later stages of the British rule in this district. There are no traces of Roman coins, Roman weapons, or any other Roman articles to be found there, so we conclude that it was abandoned before the Romans came to Britain, and, indeed, before trade with Rome was at all general. Hence if we say that the *dun* was inhabited in about 200 B.C., we shall not be very far wrong.

What is now left of this old British fort is a round enclosure, about three to four hundred feet in diameter, surrounded by a wide and deep ditch, above which are the remains of an earthern rampart. No doubt this rampart was originally much higher and stronger, and we may imagine that it was crowned by some kind of wooden stockade, but of this naturally nothing is left.

An error very common, even at the present day, is the idea that, before the Romans came, the inhabitants of this island were savages in a very low state of civilisation. The relics discovered on Hunsbury Hill show that the dwellers there, though probably an extremely war-like race, were in many respects far from being savages. Among the remains we have stone spindle-whorls and other implements for spinning and weaving, bone needles, bronze rings and buckles, iron saws, chisels, knives, nails, and sickles. The charred remnants of three different kinds of corn tell us that the inhabitants of the *dun* were well advanced in agricultural knowledge. There are several hundred pieces of pottery, much of it designed and decorated in a way that shows that these Britons possessed a fine artistic sense. There are also arms of all kinds in abundance, mostly made of iron, although one particularly good piece of work is a beautifully engraved scabbard of bronze. No British burial urns, that is, urns in which the ashes of the dead were buried, have been found on the hill, but a fair number have been discovered near Duston. It seems that the Britons took the remains of the dead down the hill and burnt the bodies there, afterwards burying the ashes in the old Neolithic village. This was not the only British burial place in the neighbourhood, there were many others ; the remains of one are to be seen within a few hundred yards of Northampton School.

There is another relic in the Museum which gives a glimpse of the more barbaric side of the dwellers on Hunsbury Hill. This is a human skull, pierced in the crown with three small holes, and it looks very much as if these holes were used to suspend this ghastly trophy outside the hut of some victorious warrior.

Other articles left in the *dun* seem to tell of a sudden abandonment of this stronghold by its inhabitants. No less than a hundred stone querns, or hand-mills for grinding corn, have been discovered there. Most of them are as fit for use to-day as they were then, so they can hardly have been thrown away; they are much too big to have been lost by accident. If the Britons had simply moved away to some other settlement, they would have taken the querns with them, heavy though they were, for much time and trouble would be necessary to obtain the stone with which to make fresh ones. It really appears that, for some reason or other, the dwellers on Hunsbury Hill were forced to fly for their lives, leaving behind their querns, the weight of which would have impeded their retreat. Why did they fly? Was it a pestilence that drove them from the spot that had been their home for so long? Was it the fear of some hostile tribe, whom they were too few to resist? Was it the rumour of the approach of the Roman legions? We cannot tell; row upon row the abandoned querns stand silently in their place in the Museum and offer us no certain solution of the mystery.

CHAPTER III.

UNDER THE ROMAN RULE.

THE first Roman invasion of this country took place in 55 B.C., when Julius Cæsar brought over an army from Gaul to teach the islanders that those who helped Rome's enemies must feel the weight of Rome's heavy hand. Neither in the first expedition, nor in the second one which took place the following year, did Cæsar make any attempt to conquer Britain. His troops never came anywhere near the Nene valley, and, although the inhabitants of this district doubtless heard tales of the valour and discipline of his legions, these first invasions had no direct effect upon the Britons who lived here.

It was not until about a hundred years later that the tide of the Roman Conquest reached our district. Claudius was then Emperor of Rome, and his generals were the first to attempt to make Britain a part of the Roman dominions. The Britons fought bravely, but they could not withstand the attacks of the well-trained legionaries by whom they were opposed. Some think that one of the great victories of Ostorius Scapula, who commanded the invading army, was won at Borough Hill, near Daventry, but this is not absolutely certain. At all events, within a few years, all Britain south of the Tyne, was in possession of the Roman army. There were occasional revolts, such as that of Boadicea, but by 90 A.D., all resistance had ceased.

The policy of the Roman was to crush without mercy those who resisted them, but, when once they had established their power over a nation, their rule was always strong and generally just. The first thing they did in Britain was to make great roads from end to end of the country, and, although the planning and designing of these roads was in the hands of their own skilled engineers, the natives were forced to do a great part of the actual work. We may be sure that the

Britons of this part of the country were obliged to perform their share of the construction of Watling Street, the greatest of the many great roads that were made at that time. It ran, and still runs, not far from Northampton, coming up from London to Towcester (or Lactodorum, as the Romans called it) and passing thence near the modern Nether Heyford and Weedon to Bannaventa, which was just north of Norton, near Daventry, and going thence to the north-west on its way to Chester.

It is easy to imagine how the Britons grumbled at the hard work imposed upon them by their foreign taskmasters, yet, though the Roman rule meant forced labour and heavy tribute, it was not without its advantages. Before the Romans came over there had been constant war, one tribe fighting against another continually, now there was complete peace. Hadrian's Great Wall kept back the savage tribes of the north from southern Britain, and, secured by the ever-watchful legions from all attacks from without, the Britons began to learn from their conquerors the arts of civilisation.

Before long, Romans other than the soldiers came to live here. Britain was never a Roman colony in the same way that Canada is an English colony ; our island must have seemed very bleak and chilly to men born in sunny Italy. Still, the various officials, merchants, and others whose business brought them here were bound to live somewhere, and in addition there must have been a few old soldiers who chose to spend the evening of their life in the land where they had served for so many years. Thus it is that we find some remains of Roman villas in this neighbourhood.

We must be quite sure that we realise exactly what a villa was. In modern England the word is used to mean quite a small house, but a Roman villa must be compared rather to a large country mansion. Fragments of tesselated pavements and other remains show that they were splendidly built, and that Roman life in the days of the Empire was very luxurious indeed. Near the villa, in which the rich owner himself lived, were lands that were cultivated by his slaves, while further off was other land belonging to the estate, in the possession of tenants called *coloni*, who paid rent for the use of it.

In Roman times there seems to have been a settlement in the vicinity of Duston, near the old Neolithic village. There are traces of villas at Harpole, Nether Heyford, Brixworth, and elsewhere. Numerous Roman articles of all kinds have been discovered in these places, the most common being coins and *fibulæ* (buckles with which the toga was fastened). A few articles have been found on the eastern side of the Nene, where Northampton Castle afterwards stood, and it is probable that some people lived there then, although it was not the actual site of a villa.

So generation after generation of Britons passed their lives under the strong rule of Rome, and, as time went on, the character of the conquered people began to change. They were no longer war-like, for, with no enemies to fear, the need for everyone to be trained to arms passed away. Britain supplied her share of recruits to help to fill the ranks of the imperial legions, but the British levies were often drafted away to serve in some other part of Rome's vast dominions. Many a man, born and bred in the Nene valley, has died fighting for Rome on the banks of the Danube or in the deserts of Parthia.

Similarly it must be remembered, when we speak of the Roman soldiers in England, that few of them were born in Rome, or even in Italy. Especially is this true of the later days of the Empire. The frontier line that Rome had to guard was so long that her rulers were forced to draw recruits from every part of the Empire, and even from the unconquered nations beyond its boundaries.

At length Rome began to totter to her fall. Saxon pirates, realising the weakness of the dying Empire, began to prey upon the eastern coast as early as 350 A.D. In 410 A.D., the crisis came. Every soldier in Britain was withdrawn to defend Rome itself, to make one final desperate effort to save the imperial city from the onslaught of the vigorous young northern nations, before whom it was destined to fall. Most of the Roman inhabitants departed from the island with the legions, and the Britons were left defenceless against the fierce barbarian tribes that threatened them on every side.

CHAPTER IV.

HOW THE ANGLO-SAXONS FOUNDED NORTHAMPTON.

WE have but few records of the troubled times that followed the departure of the Romans, and we will not here try to trace the history of the next two hundred years from the scanty materials that do exist. Let it suffice that by the end of that time Britain had fallen a prey to the Jutes, Angles, and Saxons, three heathen tribes who came from the country near the mouth of the Elbe, in North Germany. These invaders belonged to the Teutonic race. The Jutes were only a small tribe, so henceforth we shall speak of all the invading tribes as Anglo-Saxons, as this is the name by which they are generally known, although, strictly speaking, the people who settled in this part of the country were Angles.

Long and bitter was the struggle before the Britons were finally driven into Cumberland, Wales, and Cornwall, where their descendants live to-day. There are great differences of opinion as to what proportion of them survived in England as subjects of their barbarian conquerors. The number cannot have been very great, for hardly any places in South-Eastern England have British names. Our language consists of many thousands of words ; of these only two hundred are of Celtic origin. These facts seem to point to an almost complete extermination of the Britons.

It is generally thought, by those who have an expert knowledge of such matters, that a much larger proportion of Britons survived in the country between the Nene and the Welland than in other districts. This conclusion is based partly upon a study of the physical peculiarities of the modern inhabitants of this part of England, and partly upon the fact that there were then dense forests and great marshes here which no doubt served as places of refuge for the defeated Britons. It is, however, very difficult to speak with any certainty on this question.

As has been said before, little is known of the details of the conquest. The Anglo-Saxons probably came up the Nene and the Welland in their small ships, for they were a sea-faring race and generally invaded this country by following the line of some river. When they established themselves here almost every trace of Roman civilisation vanished. The Anglo-Saxons had never come under the Roman influence at all, and in consequence were quite uncivilised, and hated the ways of civilised people.

All over the countryside the Anglo-Saxon villages arose. Sometimes they called the village a " ham " or " home," as at Rockingham, sometimes a " tun," which means a settlement, as at Brington, sometimes the clan that made their home in a place gave it their family name, as at Billing. In places where they found an old Roman *castra*, they usually gave their settlement a name ending in " cester," as at Towcester.

At some time or other, we cannot say exactly when, a body of Anglo-Saxon settlers resolved to make their home upon the left bank of the Nene, on the spot where the parish of St. Peter's is to-day. Here these flaxen-haired, blue-eyed barbarians set to work to erect for themselves a village, and before long they had settled down in what they considered comfort, though most people of the present day would have thought their dwellings the reverse of comfortable.

They called this village Hamtune, " the home settlement." Thus it was that our town began its life. Not till many years later was it necessary to call it Northamtune, to distinguish it from the other " home settlement " in the south.

As the years passed on, changes took place in the character of the Anglo-Saxons. They again became what their ancestors had been in their old home in Germany, before necessity had driven them overseas to seek a new country, a stolid, plodding race of farmers, greatly attached to the homes they had built and to the land that gave them food. They were not very quick-witted, they were extremely obstinate, they were slow of speech and rough in their ways ; but they had within them the qualities that have made their descendants rulers of a great world-empire.

At first this district was part of Mercia, one of the several kingdoms into which England was then divided. Mercia, under Penda, was the last kingdom to attempt to uphold by force of arms the old pagan worship of Woden and Thor against Christianity, but after the death of Penda in 655, the conversion of the Mercians was more rapid than that of any other people had been. All Mercia was formed into one great bishopric, the centre of which was Lichfield.

Meanwhile there was a constant struggle for supremacy between the different kingdoms. For a long time Mercia and Wessex fought with one another over this question, and once Mercia had the upper hand, but at last Wessex prevailed, and all England owned the overlordship of Egbert.

How these changes affected the Anglo-Saxons who dwelt in Hamtune is uncertain, for not until the 10th century is our town mentioned in any written record that we still possess. It is equally hard to give any detailed account of their ordinary daily life here.

Probably most of the people in Hamtune worked on the land, but some simple industries would be carried on in many of the houses. Every building in the town was of wood, except the churches. Of these there were at least two in existence before the Norman Conquest, one on the site of St. Peter's, and the other on that of St. Sepulchre's. Both were rebuilt by the Normans, but there are traces of Saxon workmanship on some of the stones in the present buildings. One of the most interesting of these stones is to be seen in the south porch of St. Sepulchre's, where it can easily be detected. There is a public path going through the churchyard; as you enter the path from Sheep Street the porch will be on your left. When you enter the porch, turn right round so as to face the entrance through which you have just come. You will then see, on the left side of the entrance and about seven feet from the floor, a stone with a circle carved upon it, with a number of lines going from the centre to the circumference. This is a Saxon sun-dial, as we know from the marks upon it and the distance between them, for the Saxon clergy divided the day into periods different from those in use afterwards.

One's first thought is, of course, "Who can have put a sun-dial in a place like that, where the sun never reaches it?" The explanation is quite simple; the sun-dial used to be outside the church. When the porch was re-built in about 1400, some workman, who found the sun-dial mixed up with the stones he was using, built it into the wall, having no idea of its original purpose.

There may also have been a church in the place where All Saints' now stands, but we cannot be certain of this. The position of a church built there would not have been at all central, for the Anglo-Saxon village would hardly have reached so far east. If there was a church on this site, it was rebuilt, like the other two, in Norman times, so we have no example left in this town of an Anglo-Saxon church. The church at Brixworth, which is in part constructed from the remains of an older Roman building, gives a good idea of what the early Anglo-Saxon churches were like, while the tower of Earls Barton Church is a fine example of their later work.

The great feature in Anglo-Saxon town life was the periodical gathering of the *moot*, or assembly of all the freemen. Here any disputes that had arisen would be settled; the assembly would decide what the custom was concerning the matter under discussion. Custom was everything then; even when they made a new law they always tried to persuade themselves that it was an old custom revived. The West Saxon kings made up codes of laws from time to time, but they would not be much observed here, if they were opposed to local custom, for, until the Normans came, there was no strong central government to say "Do this," and to see that it was done.

At the *moot*, too, criminals would be brought to trial. There was no police system then, but everybody had somebody else responsible for bringing him to justice if he did wrong. The accused man might escape punishment if he could get enough neighbours to swear that he was innocent; the number necessary depended upon the nature of the offence. In Northampton, the oaths were made in St. Peter's Church from the earliest times. This ceremony was called compurgation.

If the accused man could not find the necessary number of compurgators, he might then try the ordeal. In this case he was required to carry a red-hot bar of iron in his hand three paces, or else to dip his hand up to the wrist in boiling water. His hand was then wrapped up in clean linen by a priest, and the bandage sealed with the seal of the Church. After three days the seals were broken, and the bandage removed. If his hand had healed he was pronounced innocent; if not, he was declared guilty and punished.

To us it appears to have been an easy matter to escape by compurgation, but it must be remembered that when the population of the country was much less, and people did not travel much, everybody in a district knew everybody else, and so it would be very hard for any obviously guilty man to find people willing to ruin their reputation by swearing that he was innocent. Moreover, an oath was a very serious matter then; the dwellers in old Hamtune were rough, unlettered, ignorant men, but they had a simple, unswerving faith in God and a deep reverence for sacred things.

As for the ordeal, it was an appeal to a higher power to intervene when the wisdom of man had failed. Of course it was a mistake; there are some things which men must decide for themselves, and the innocence or guilt of those accused of crime is one of them. To us it seems unlikely that a burn or scald would heal in so short a time. Perhaps when men lived a hardy outdoor life their skins were tougher and their flesh healthier. Men must have undergone the ordeal successfully sometimes; if they had never been acquitted through it, others would have ceased to demand to be tried by it.

So our Anglo-Saxon ancestors lived their hard, simple, manly lives in the river-side village that is now a crowded town. They gradually became less barbarous than they had been at first, and under the influence of the Church some degree of refinement crept into their ways. To the last, though, they were unspoiled by any kind of luxury ; they were always too hard rather than too soft in their lives. Perhaps it was as well for them that such was the case, for they lived in troublous times, as the next chapter will show.

CHAPTER V.

THE DANES.

SHORTLY before the year 800, the Anglo-Saxon chroniclers begin to record continual attacks upon the coast-line of England by Scandinavian pirates. These raiders are generally spoken of as the Danes, though in all probability many of them came from Norway. They did not long rest content with mere coast raids, but began to extend their depredations inland. Finally they landed on the east coast in vast numbers, resolved to effect a permanent settlement in our country, and at one time it appeared probable that the whole island would be overrun by these heathen invaders.

Alfred the Great saved England from the Danish peril. After his great victory at Ethandune in 878, the Danes were glad to sign the Peace of Wedmore, by which they were allowed to settle in that part of England which lay to the north-east of Watling Street. Hamtune was just within the territory allotted to them, which was called the Danelaw.

The Danes settled here in large numbers. They generally gave their villages names ending in "by" or "thorp." We at once think of Long Buckby, Wilby, Althorp, and Kingsthorpe. It seems that there were a great many of them in Hamtune itself, as will be seen later.

When Alfred died in 901, the task of keeping the Danelaw under control fell to his son, Edward the Elder, who succeeded him. It was no easy matter, for, though the Danes had now settled down on the land, and many of them had become Christians, the instinct of the pirate was still strong within them. From time to time they resumed their old plundering habits and sallied forth upon some raid against their Anglo-Saxon neighbours. Fortunately Edward was a strong and capable ruler and was able eventually to suppress these lawless plunderers.

Now we come to the earliest mention of Northampton in the Anglo-Saxon Chronicle. Under the year 914 the following entry appears :—

"In this year the Danes rode out after Easter from Hamtune and from Leicester and slew many men at Hockerton (?) and thereabouts. And very soon after that the one came home, then they raised another troop which rode out against Leighton, and then were the country people ware of them and fought against them and put them to full flight and rescued all that they had taken and also a great portion of their horses and weapons."

From this passage it would seem that Hamtune was then in the possession of the Danes. They were more quick-witted than the Anglo-Saxons, though both were branches of the same Teutonic stock, and they were quick to perceive the advantages of using horses in war. Like the Anglo-Saxons, they generally fought on foot, as thus they could wield their heavy double-edged axes with more terrible effect. They realised, however, that horses were useful in land-fighting for the same reason that their swift ships had been useful in their raids on the coasts in the old days ; because, by their aid, they could make sudden and unexpected attacks upon places where they were least expected, and be gone again before people in the neighbourhood had had time to gather together to resist them. So, mounted on horses, they had ridden off to raid Hockerton. Before the slow, stolid Anglo-Saxons could gather together to resist them, the Danes had killed many men and ridden off again with their booty. Their success caused their downfall, for, flushed with their triumph, they tried another raid later in the year in the same locality. This time the Anglo-Saxons were on their guard ; at the first news of their approach the country people flocked in on all sides, armed and ready to repel the daring raiders. What little plunder the Danes had already secured was re-captured, and they were forced to retreat in confusion, leaving behind many of their horses and weapons.

Next year, Edward brought a large force into Buckinghamshire, evidently with a view to preventing any further raids into that county. For four weeks he lay encamped at Buckingham itself, fortifying the town so as to make it a stronghold from which he could operate against future disturbers of the peace. These measures seem to have made some of the Hamtune Danes think that discretion was the better part of valour, and they went to Buckingham and there sought Edward's pardon.

For a few years after this we read of no more Danish raids in this neighbourhood. Early in 921, however, there seem to have been signs of unrest once again, for, just before Easter, Edward gave orders to proceed to Towcester and to make it ready for defence against a possible attack. He was none too soon in taking this precaution, for, later in the year, while the king was engaged in suppressing a rebellion in EastAnglia, a body of Danes from Hamtune and Leicester made a sudden assault upon Towcester, hoping to take it by storm. For a whole day a desperate fight went on around the village, but, when darkness fell, the Danes were forced to retire, and the gallant little band of inhabitants waited anxiously for the dawn, which they thought would herald a new attack. When morning came, however, a relieving force that had been gathered together from the country round made its appearance, and the Danes, unable to face these new foes, made good their retreat.

They were not yet disposed to cease their marauding expeditions, and a short time after their failure at Towcester they made a sudden night raid into Buckinghamshire. This took the Saxons by surprise, and the Danes carried off many men and cattle from the neighbourhood of Aylesbury and got home again unmolested.

Edward, who by this time had subdued the East Anglian rebels, resolved to put an end to these continual raids. With a large army of trusty warriors, he marched up to Towcester. Taking up a position at Passenham to cover his operations, he sent some of his men to help the inhabitants of Towcester to surround their home with a stone wall in order to prevent any future assaults from being successful. The presence of this great army warned the Danes that any attempt to continue their lawless courses must end in their destruction. So Thurnferth, the *jarl* who commanded the Hamtune Danes, and all his followers, surrendered to Edward, "and sought him as their lord and protector." The supremacy of the West Saxon king was assured, every Danish stronghold from the Nene to the Welland fell into his hands, and thenceforth the countryside had peace.

The kings who followed Edward the Elder continued his work, and gradually Dane and Anglo-Saxon blended together. After all, they were of the same race originally, though long centuries spent in the cold North had quickened the Dane's wits and had also made him rather more cruel and relentless than his Anglo-Saxon cousin. Under Dunstan's able rule, the Anglo-Saxon kingdom reached the height of its power.

At last, in 979, Ethelred the Redeless ascended the throne. This "king without counsel" brought to ruin the whole work of his predecessors. The Danes again harried the coasts, bribes failed to keep them away, and, finally, the terrible massacre of St. Brice's Day brought over Sweyn with a formidable host of warriors, eager to avenge the cruel folly of Ethelred. Hamtune was one of the places that fell victims to his wrath, for in 1010 he attacked it and burnt it to the ground.

It does not seem to have been long before fresh houses were built, and the peaceful reign of Canute gave Hamtune an opportunity to recover from the effects of this disaster. As we have no idea when the Anglo-Saxon churches were built, we can say nothing certain about what happened to them when Sweyn destroyed the town.

For fifty years after this no foes from without disturbed the Hamtune burgesses; then again the town was ravaged with fire and sword.

In 1065, when Edward the Confessor was upon the throne, and Harold, afterwards king of England, was ruling the realm for the pious old man, trouble arose in Northumbria. Tostig, Harold's brother, was the earl who ruled that part, and the people there, who hated him, rose in arms and drove him from his earldom. They chose Morcar as earl in his stead, and under his leadership, a great body of Northumbrains marched south till they came to Hamtune. To a Mercian, a Northumbrian was still a foreigner, and it is easy to imagine the dismay of the inhabitants as company after company of the northern rebels marched into the little town. Their fears were unfortunately only too well grounded. Morcar's brother, Edwin, joined him here with his Mercian levies, and a number of Britons from Wales. To this rebel host came Harold, sent by the king to see if a civil war could be avoided. The three earls held a council, and finally Harold went back to the king to see if he would consent to the deposition of Tostig. While he was away, the wild northerners, impatient at the long delay, began to pillage and burn the houses in the town. Edwin and Morcar either would not, or could not, restrain their followers, whose help they would need if Edward refused to yield to their demand for Tostig's deposition. The northerners therefore slew men, burnt houses, and destroyed corn all over the countryside, " so that the shire and all the other shires which are nigh were for many winters the worse." At last, Harold returned, and the whole force went off to Oxford, where they held another council, and it was decided that Tostig must give up his earldom and go into exile.

The events of the next year are better known than those of any other year in our nation's history—how Harold seized the throne when Edward the Confessor died, how he had to face an invasion by Tostig and his Norwegian allies in the north and another by William of Normandy in the south, how Tostig fought and fell at Stamford Bridge, and, finally, how Harold, last of the Anglo-Saxon kings, died beneath the dragon flag of Wessex, as the sun set upon the terrible battle-field near Hastings, on which was ended for ever the rule of the House of Godwin.

CHAPTER VI.

THE NORMAN CONQUEST.

THE battle of Hastings marked the beginning and not the end of William's conquest of England. The Anglo-Saxons were very slow to awake to the fact that a foreign ruler had seated himself upon the throne. When they did realise this, rebellions broke out in every part of the country, but there was no united action; district after district rose against the Normans, district after district was subdued in turn. Moreover, the Anglo-Saxon leaders mistrusted one another (generally not without reason), while the new king was a born soldier and a great statesman. By 1071, the storming of Hereward's camp of refuge at Ely had ended all open resistance.

The problem which William I. and his successors had to face was a difficult one. All probability of a successful Anglo-Saxon rising soon vanished, but the real danger came from the Normans, not from the Anglo-Saxons. Those who had risked life, money, and men in the expedition that had proved so successful, now looked for a substantial reward. William, they thought, would grant to each of them a generous portion of the conquered land, which they would rule, nominally as his vassals, really as independent princes. Then they could oppress their Anglo-Saxon subjects to their hearts' content, live comfortably on the revenues extracted from them, and enliven the monotony of life by occasional brisk little wars among themselves.

William, however, knew from his own personal experience how easily a powerful baron in France could make himself practically independent of the king who was supposed to be his over-lord, and he did not intend anything of the kind to occur in England. He was quite willing to grant the lands of the conquered Saxons to his Norman followers, but he took very good care not to give too much to any one man in the same part of the country. He did not mean to permit the existence of any semi-independent baronies; his intention was to be king, not merely in name, but in reality.

Hence, for many years, William and his successors were occupied with a continual struggle against their barons, which sometimes broke out into actual warfare. Strange though it may seem, it was this very circumstance that aided the rise of Northampton to importance. In their efforts to establish completely their supremacy over the whole country, the kings of this period were naturally attracted to any place that was centrally situated, whither they could easily summon their followers from all parts, and whence they could strike swiftly at any point where rebellion threatened to break out. In many ways Northampton was ideally suited for their purpose. It was about half way between Winchester, the old capital of Wessex, and York, the chief city of Northumbria. While fairly near London and the ports whence Normandy could be reached, it was also not too far from the Welsh and Scottish borders. Apart from considerations of this nature, it was then situated near a great forest, in which the rulers of England were able to enjoy the pleasures of the chase, so dear to the hearts of almost all the kings of that time.

So, for about 300 years, Northampton was one of the favourite residences of the kings of England. This was not entirely due to its central position and other similar advantages. To some extent the town's rapid rise in importance resulted from these, but some of its progress was due to the Norman earl who ruled here, and of whom we shall speak anon. By a striking coincidence, Northampton came under the influence of a man well able to develop its possibilities at the very moment when its natural position and the political conditions of the time made it suitable for a royal residence. This combination of circumstances soon made Northampton one of the leading towns of England.

It will be noticed that we now speak no longer of Hamtune, but of Northampton, for such is the name given to our town in Domesday Book. The entry relating to Northampton says that in Edward the Confessor's time there had been sixty houses here, fourteen of which were now "waste." (This is a grim reminder of the deeds of Morcar's Northumbrians). At the time the Domesday Book was compiled, that is, in about 1086, Northampton consisted of over 300 houses. This points to a very rapid growth, which seems to have continued apace during the years that followed, if we may judge anything from the area enclosed by the first wall that was built round the town shortly afterwards.

Now let us turn from the town for a moment and see what Domesday Book says about one of the villages near here. Almost every village in this neighbourhood was enrolled in this great survey of the land. A typical example will help us to understand more clearly the manner in which our ancestors lived in the country districts in those days.

Weston Favell was then a "manor" or estate which was held by Robert, Count of Mortain. This Robert was a half-brother of William the Conqueror, and held many other manors, which were scattered all over England. William, as we have said, was always careful not to give any of his barons too much land in one place. Robert probably visited Weston Favell from time to time, but he did not live there. The manor was managed for him by a bailiff, who would be under the supervision of another official of Robert's, called a seneschal, who had to look after all the manors held by his lord in this part of the country. The entry in Domesday Book is as follows:

"The land of the Count of Mortain.

In Weston Favell the Count holds 2½ hides. There is land for five ploughs. In demesne there are 2 ploughs and 4 bondmen. And there are 12 villeins and 2 bordars with 3½ ploughs. There are ten acres of meadow. It was worth 40s.: it is now worth 60s. Leuric held it freely".

A hide was, roughly speaking, about 120 acres, so Robert's estate at Weston Favell contained something like 300 acres of cultivated land. In the centre of the estate was the manor-house, and around it the huts of the villeins, bordars, and bondmen. As a rule the manor-house was a centre where four roads met, each going off across the estate in a different direction We may imagine the Weston Favell manor-house to be situated about where the cross roads are to-day. All around, the land of the manor lay open to the view; there were no hedges then.

The whole of the cultivated land was divided into three great fields. Every year, wheat, which is sown in the autumn, was grown in one field, barley or oats, which are sown in the spring, in another, and the third was left fallow, in order that the ground might recover its fertility. Of course, a different field was left fallow each year.

In each field the land was split up into numerous small strips of about an acre or half an acre. These strips were divided from one another by balks of unploughed turf. In this manor a little over a quarter of the whole number of strips were cultivated for Robert, under the management of his bailiff; these strips were called the demesne land. The remainder of the land was divided up among the villeins and bordars. The principal difference between these two classes was that the bordars had much less land than the villiens.

Now, a word as to the position of these villeins and bordars. They were not exactly freemen, nor were they actually slaves, as the four bondmen were. They could not leave the manor and had to pay various small dues to Robert from time to time. In addition, they each had to do two days work in the week upon the demesne land, and extra work there at harvest time.. Thus Robert had four villeins working for him every day, and for four days in the week one of the bordars also, besides his four slaves. Robert had two ploughs for use on the demesne; these would be drawn by oxen. One of the villeins, who was called the reeve, was a kind of foreman, and had to see that the others did the work allotted to them.

Robert paid these men no wages, but when they were not engaged on his demesne they could work on their own strips of land, whence they derived their living. A villein's strips were not all together, they were situated in different parts of the three big fields, about an equal number being in each. They were separated in this way, because, if a man had all his strips in one field, he would be very awkwardly placed in the year in which that field was left fallow. Moreover, the quality of land varied very much then, and it would have been unfair for one man to have all good land and another all bad land, so each had some strips of the good land and some of the bad. Sometimes, of course, the lord of the manor included all the best land in his demesne.

Besides the arable land of the manor there was Robert's meadow, which was used for growing hay, and also a piece of rough, untilled ground, known as the "waste," upon which the oxen of lord and villein alike grazed, and which everyone on the manor could use for obtaining turf or gathering fuel.

Such was the manor that Robert, Count of Mortain, possessed near Northampton, at the time when Domesday Book was compiled. The manor had brought in about 40s. a year in Edward the Confessor's reign; it now brought in half as much again. It is difficult to estimate exactly the value of money in those days, but, if we reckon every penny to be worth about two shillings, we shall have a fairly accurate idea of its purchasing power. Robert, for the privilege of holding this manor and the others that he possessed elsewhere, undertook to supply the king with a certain number of fully armed and equipped knights for forty days in the year, if the king needed their services.

Where was Leuric now, the sturdy Saxon who had held the manor "freely" when the Confessor sat on the throne? Was his body one of those that had lain piled up in the ghastly heap around King Harold's corpse on Senlac Hill? Was he still alive, an exile in some distant part of Europe? No one can say; at all events he had lost his land, and probably his life with it.

So we have in Weston Favell a typical example of how William gave English land to his Norman followers, and of how they managed the estates they thus acquired. The town itself was not at first given into the charge of a Norman baron. Waltheof, the first Earl of Northampton, one of the few surviving Anglo-Saxon nobles, ruled here during the greater part of William's reign. He had participated in one of the earlier rebellions against William, but had been pardoned and was now married to Judith, the Conqueror's niece.

Waltheof was a man of great physical strength and had shown himself to be a gallant soldier, but he was as weak of will as he was strong of body. Towards the end of the reign he allowed himself to be implicated in a plot formed against William by two Norman barons, and, although he was the least guilty of the three, William ordered him to be executed. Perhaps the king was not sorry to have this opportunity of ridding himself of the last of the Anglo-Saxon nobility, for now his power was well established, and he no longer needed to conciliate the conquered nation.

Waltheof left a daughter, Matilda by name. Early in the reign of William Rufus, she was married to a Norman baron called Simon de Senlis. It is said that Simon's first intention was to marry Waltheof's widow, Judith, but that she rejected him because he was lame in one foot. Whether this be true or not, Simon de Senlis married her daughter. He thus became Earl of Northampton, and his elevation to that position opens a new epoch in the history of the town.

CHAPTER VII.

SIMON DE SENLIS.

IT was a fortunate day for our town when Simon de Senlis became Earl of Northampton. Very little is known of his personal character, but, whatever faults he may have had, he was undoubtedly a capable and energetic man, firmly resolved that the town entrusted to his care should be made one worthy to rank beside any other in England. When we think of some of the barons of that period, men who seemed to have no other ambition than to plunder and destroy, men whose cruelty and wickedness were a bye-word even in that iron age, we realise how happy a chance it was that brought our town under the influence of Simon de Senlis.

It is probable that the Anglo-Saxon inhabitants disliked the idea of a foreign earl, though perhaps the fact that Simon was the husband of Waltheof's daughter may have reconciled them to his rule. For Waltheof, in spite of his weak character, had become a popular hero after his death. For years the Anglo-Saxons talked of him and told one another stories of the dead earl. Some were true, such as the tale of how he had held the gate of York single-handed against the Normans, how the huge battle-axe that he wielded had cloven man after man through helmet and through head, until the surviving foemen had shrunk back in terror from the mighty Anglo-Saxon warrior. Some were false legends; of these the best known is the tale that, when he was beheaded, the executioner smote Waltheof's head from his shoulders while the earl was kneeling to say the Lord's Prayer for the last time, and that the severed head completed the prayer that had been interrupted by the fatal stroke. True or false, the Anglo-Saxons firmly believed these stories, and perhaps found in them some consolation for their own hard lot.

Indeed, they had much to endure of which they might well complain. The Normans had brought their own customs with them and enforced them rigorously. Moreover, there was now on the throne a king who was determined that his laws should be observed throughout all England. Many changes had consequently taken place in the daily life of the Northampton townsfolk. The cruel forest laws, which inflicted terrible penalties upon all who interfered with the king's deer, must have affected the people of Northampton to some extent, as a royal forest was so near the town. The taxes were much heavier than ever before; there were all sorts of new dues to be paid. Again, the curfew bell, which is to us merely a quaint old relic of a half-forgotten past, was to them the new and tyrannical device of a foreign conqueror.

Another law which was heartily detested was that which made the whole district responsible if a Norman was murdered there and his slayer escaped. This was intended to prevent the Anglo-Saxons from avenging their wrongs by assassination. It led to great injustice, for whenever the body of an unknown murdered man was found in Northampton (by no means an uncommon occurrence in those times of bloodshed and violence), all the people in the town were fined unless they could prove conclusively that the corpse was not that of a Norman.

Trials, too, were not conducted in the same way that they had been. The Normans, instead of employing the ordeal, introduced the system of trial by battle. Accused and accuser fought until one or the other yielded or was killed. As in the ordeal, it was believed that God would distinguish between the innocent and the guilty. It was in many ways a grossly unfair test, owing to the difference in personal strength and skill that might exist between the two men. Moreover, although in criminal cases the accuser and accused fought in person, in civil lawsuits a champion could be hired to fight on behalf of either side, a custom that operated very harshly against the poor. It was little wonder that the Anglo-Saxons hated the attempts of their conquerors to force this custom upon them, for the old ordeal, though far from being an ideal method of determining between innocence and guilt, at least offered the same chance of escape to all accused persons.

So Simon de Senlis had by no means a contented and happy populace with which to deal. Yet we hear nothing of riots or trouble at Northampton during his lifetime. Such was his firmness and tact that, in spite of the natural dislike felt by the Saxons towards a foreign ruler, Simon's earldom was marked by continued peace and progress.

Simon's first care was to build a castle. He selected as its site the position that is occupied to-day by the London and North-Western Railway Company's Goods Shed. Here the Castle was erected upon a large mound. On three sides it was surrounded by a moat, on the fourth it was protected by the river. It must be remembered that the course of the Nene was diverted by the Railway Company about thirty years ago ; in Norman times it flowed more to the east and ran right over the site of the modern station.

The Great Gate of the Castle stood in what is now St. Andrew's Road, near the door leading to the garden of St. Peter's Rectory. Here a drawbridge crossed the moat, being protected on the outer side by a barbican, or small outwork. If a sudden surprise attack carried the barbican before the drawbridge could be drawn up, there was a portcullis above the Great Gate which could be let down at once to prevent the assailants from entering the Castle.

This Great Gate was built in a lofty wall which stood above the moat or river on every side. At least eight towers of various sizes stood at different points along this wall. Within the circle of the wall were the buildings that composed the castle proper. Of these, the most important was the Keep, a massive tower which overlooked the whole town and much of the surrounding country.

To this day such names as Castle Station, Castle Street, and Castle Hill remind us of the days when the huge Norman stronghold towered upon its lofty mound above the wooden houses and narrow streets of old Northampton. Of the actual fabric there still remains one postern gate. It was taken from the wall of the old Castle and built, stone by stone, into the wall surrounding the grounds of Warner's Hotel. You will find it on your right, a few yards beyond the entrance to the Goods Department, as you go from the centre of the town towards the Castle Station.

Simon was a great builder, and he did not rest content when he had erected the Castle, but further protected the growing town by surrounding it with a wall. The area enclosed by this wall gives some idea of the size of Northampton then. South of the Castle, the west side of which formed part of the wall, was the West Gate, situated a short distance nearer the centre of the town than the bridge over the Nene. From the West Gate the wall ran in a south-easterly direction, keeping north of the river and of the modern gas-works, near which was a postern gate, until it came to Bridge Street, where stood the South Gate, a little below St. John's Hospital. Then the wall went east, along the line of Cattle Market Road, until it came to the bottom of what is now called Swan Street. This was then known as Cow Lane and led down to the Cow Gate, through which the townsfolk drove their cattle out to Cow Meadow. After passing Cow Gate, the wall curved in a more northerly direction and came to Derngate. Here, as the name indicates, was the Water Gate, then flanked by a lofty building known as the Tower, of which nothing now remains. Passing on, the wall crossed St. Giles' street, where there was a postern gate. Outside the gate lay the site of St. Giles' Church, which was built some few years later. Then the wall went north until it came to Abington Street, which then ended near the modern Convent, beyond which was the East Gate. Still going north, the wall crossed Lady's Lane, and then, passing along the line of the Upper Mounts, it came to the North Gate, just above the present Regent Square After this the wall ran nearly due west until it reached the river, which formed a natural defence to the town on its western side.

Simon's zeal for building did not end with the completion of these defensive works. He either built or rebuilt All Saints' Church ; it is impossible to say which, as we do not know for certain whether it existed in Saxon times. The modern church still contains portions of a Norman arch, but, as it was greatly altered about the time of Henry III., and almost entirely destroyed by fire in the reign of Charles II., the building which we see to-day bears no resemblance to that erected by Simon.

It is now that we first hear of the Priory of St. Andrew, though some have claimed a Saxon origin for this, too. The general opinion is, however, that it was founded by Simon de Senlis. At all events, in about 1094, he endowed it richly, bestowing large grants of land upon it and giving it the patronage of all the churches of the town. This priory, which from now until the Reformation figures prominently in the history of the town, was a large building situated near the North Gate, and to the north-west of Regent Square. The town wall was extended here to include the Priory within its circumference. It was in the possession of the Cluniac monks, a foreign brotherhood, and the prior was generally a Frenchman. Priory Street, Monk's Pond Street, and other names of a similar nature in this locality still recall to our minds the existence of this religious house, though all traces of the once famous building have passed away.

Simon de Senlis' activities were by no means confined to Northampton. In addition to his work here, he lived the ordinary life of a baron under the Norman kings. In 1096, when Peter the Hermit's preaching had stirred all Europe with the desire to free the Holy Sepulchre from the infidel Saracens, Simon was among those who took the cross and sailed to the Holy Land upon the First Crusade. He cannot have stayed there until the capture of Jerusalem, for in 1098 we find him fighting for William II. in Normandy against Philip I., of France. Here Simon was taken prisoner, but he seems to have got back to England soon after, so, presumably, he was exchanged or ransomed. Perhaps it was partly in gratitude for his safe return, partly to commemorate his expedition to Palestine, that he built the Church of the Holy Sepulchre at Northampton. Unlike All Saints' Church, this building has still many features which tell us of its Norman origin. The massive pillars, that stand in the circular part of the church, are typically Norman, although the round arches that were once above them have disappeared. There are few circular churches left in England to-day; this form of architecture was imitated from the original Church of the Holy Sepulchre at Jerusalem.

The Norman baron did not live long after he had completed this last achievement. A few years later he made another journey to Palestine and visited Jerusalem, now in the hands of the Crusaders, and the capital of a short-lived kingdom. On his way back he died, while passing through France, and was buried in the Priory of St. Mary de Charité-sur-Loire.

Simon de Senlis was dead, but his work remained. He had found Northampton an obscure provincial town; he left it a place worthy of the important part it was destined to play in the history of our country.

CHAPTER VIII.

THE LATER NORMAN KINGS.

SIMON de Senlis left two sons, both of whom were minors at the time of their father's death. The Earldom of Northampton passed to Prince David of Scotland, who married Simon's widow, Matilda. Henry I. naturally did not allow Northampton Castle to fall into the hands of a foreign prince, but took possession of it himself.

Henceforth Northampton Castle was one of the principal royal strongholds. Every English king from Henry I. to Edward III. visited it at least once, and most of them stayed there for some time.

The first recorded royal visit to our town took place in 1106, when Henry I. met Robert of Normandy at the Castle. On that occasion a last attempt was made to settle peacefully the questions at issue between the royal brothers. In 1122 Henry held his court at the Castle and celebrated Easter with great pomp. About nine years later he was here again, and our town was then the scene of a most important historical event.

By this time, the Norman kings seemed at last to have established their supremacy over the unruly barons. Robert of Normandy, the last hope of the party of disorder, was a prisoner for life in Cardiff Castle, his leading supporters were mostly banished, in prison, or dead, and Normandy itself, ever the refuge of past disturbers of peace, was now in possession of Henry I. Travelling justices were doing something to bring into existence one system of law for the whole of England, though local custom was still strong. Yet, in spite of the seeming strength of the royal position, thoughtful men looked ahead with apprehension. Henry's only son, William, had been drowned in the White Ship; the king's daughter, Matilda was haughty and little liked; his nephew, Stephen of Blois, was popular with all men. Would the barons submit to the rule of Matilda? Would Matilda suffer the crown to be taken from her without a desperate struggle? The outlook for the future seemed gloomy indeed.

None realised the state of affairs more fully than Henry I. Wearied by his life-long struggle for power, heart-broken by the loss of his dearly loved son, he foresaw only too well the troubles that must follow his own death, which could not now be long delayed. Henry resolved to do all that lay in his power to secure the peaceful accession of Matilda, and accordingly he summoned to Northampton all the great lords of his kingdom.

So, in 1131, Northampton was filled with the numerous retainers and attendants who had followed the nobility of England in their journey to our town. When all the barons had arrived, the ceremony for which they had been gathered together took place. One by one, the great nobles of England knelt before the Empress Matilda, as she stood by the high altar of old All Saints' Church, placed their rough, war-hardened hands between the delicate white palms of the royal lady, and solemnly repeated the feudal oath of allegiance.

"Hear, my lady! I do become liege man of yours of life and limb, and of earthly worship, and faith and truth I will bear unto you, to live or die, against all manner of folk. So help me God."

What Henry could do to secure the throne for his daughter, he had done, but even the restraint of an oath was not enough to check the ambition of Stephen and his supporters.

In 1135 Henry died. "May God give him the peace that he loved," writes the chronicler. For England, Henry's death meant not peace but anarchy. A terrible civil war broke out between Stephen's adherents and those of Matilda. Neither claimant, engrossed as each was in the fierce struggle for power, had a moment's thought to spare for the good of the kingdom. The nobility, knowing themselves to be safe from interference, broke loose from all restraint. Everywhere robber strongholds arose, and from these the barons plundered, slaughtered, and burnt in all directions. "Men said that Christ and His saints slept."

Amid all this strife and misery, Northampton, protected by its strong castle and lofty walls, remained unscathed. The citizens must have blessed the foresight and energy of Simon de Senlis when tales of the sad fate of unprotected towns and villages came to their ears. They realised then how completely they owed their security to the work of the dead earl. In that time of terror, the mere sight of two or three horsemen on the horizon was enough to make the inhabitants of an unfortified place abandon their homes and fly for their lives.

Meanwhile, the sons of Simon de Senlis had both grown to manhood. The younger of the two, who was named Waltheof, does not come very much into the history of the town. At quite an early age he entered the Church, greatly to the annoyance of his elder brother. After some years, Waltheof became an abbot, and gained a great reputation for piety. He is said to have been offered the Archbishopric of York, and to have refused it. After his death, miracles were reported to have been worked at his tomb. Eventually he was canonised and thus became St. Waltheof.

The elder son of Simon de Senlis bore the same name as his father. To prevent confusion, he will hereafter be referred to as Simon de Senlis II. Some such method of distinction is necessary, as the first Simon's Christian name was given, not only to his son, but also to his grandson and great-grandson.

Simon de Senlis II. was described by Robert of Gloucester as "one whose acts never got beyond speech, nor his gifts beyond promises." Robert was undoubtedly prejudiced against him on personal grounds; what we know of Simon's life does not bear out this description. He was a staunch supporter of Stephen throughout the civil war and fought on the king's side at the battle of Lincoln. His loyalty gained for him the Earldom of Northampton. David, who had previously held the title, had now become King of Scotland. In 1138, he had led an army into England to help the Empress Matilda, but had been defeated at Northallerton. Doubtless Stephen held that David had forfeited his earldom by this action, for in the year 1141 Simon de Senlis II. is described as the Earl of Northampton.

Like his father, Simon de Senlis II. was a great builder. He founded De La Pré Abbey and endowed it richly. A body of Cluniac nuns lived there until the reign of Henry VIII., when the abbey shared the fate of the other religious houses in the country. Nothing is now left of the original buildings. It was the proximity of this convent that gave to Nunn Mills the name which they still bear.

At this point we may mention one or two other buildings which were certainly in existence during the earlier half of the 12th century, although the exact date of their foundation is unknown. St. Giles' Church is mentioned as early as 1120; there were as many as nine Northampton churches in existence at that date. Early in Stephen's reign, St. John's Hospital was founded for the reception of the aged and infirm poor. The chapel formerly attached to this building still stands in Bridge Street; it is of somewhat later date than the original hospital. Further down the road, a little beyond the point where the railway now crosses it, stood St. Leonard's Hospital, where dwelt those unhappy men who had been smitten with the terrible plague of leprosy.

Throughout the civil war, Northampton Castle was held for Stephen and does not seem to have been attacked by the adherents of Matilda. The king himself was constantly at Northampton, and in 1146 an incident of some importance took place here. The details are rather obscure, but what seems to have happened is this.

Ranulf, Earl of Chester, a powerful baron on the Welsh border, came to Northampton with a few followers and sought an interview with the king. He wished Stephen to come in person to help him to repel the raids of the Welsh. The royal presence on the border, he said, would undoubtedly be a great encouragement to the English and would spread terror among their foes. Stephen, always easily persuaded by any flatterer, seemed inclined to go, but some of the king's barons began to be suspicious. The Earl of Chester had once been a prominent supporter of Matilda, though he had recently changed sides.

He had fought in her army at Lincoln, indeed, Stephen had there felled him to the earth with that last heavy blow, which had shattered the royal axe and left the king defenceless. Suppose that Ranulf intended to change sides again! Suppose that his anxiety for the king's presence was merely a pretext to entice Stephen into his power! Inquiries were made, and, as a result, the earl was imprisoned in a dungeon in the Castle. It is doubtful whether he was really plotting treachery; some writers of the time thought that he was most unfairly treated. Whether he was guilty or not on this occasion, what we know of his character in other respects is enough to convince us that his imprisonment was not altogether unmerited. Unfortunately, Stephen let him go, on condition that he swore to give up all his castles. Afterwards, as the chronicler tells us, "Some he gave up and some not, and he did then worse than before."

At last, the Treaty of Wallingford ended the civil war in 1153. In the same year Simon de Senlis II. died, and his son Simon de Senlis III. became Earl of Northampton. A year later came the death of Stephen and the opening of the eventful reign of Henry II.

NORTHAMPTON CASTLE. (General View of Old Wall and Bastion, looking N. E.).
Reproduced from The Rev. R. M. Serjeantson's "Castle of Northampton," by permission of the Author, and the Northants. Natural History Society.

CHAPTER IX.

THOMAS BECKET.

HENRY II., the first of the Plantagenet kings, was one of the most remarkable men that ever sat on the English throne. A short, strongly-built, thick-set, red-faced Angevin, he possessed at once the most able brain, the most energetic disposition, and the most ungovernable temper of any man of his time. This is not the place to enter into the details of his extraordinary career ; we have here merely to consider his actions as they affected Northampton.

As we have seen, the task of the Norman kings had been to prevent the barons from becoming semi-independent robber princes. In this they had succeeded, until the civil war in Stephen's reign had led to the breakdown of the whole machinery of government, and, in consequence, to the momentary triumph of the barons. Henry II. had now before him the work of re-establishing order in a country that had been allowed to drift into a condition of utter lawlessness.

The wonderful rapidity with which the new king accomplished his difficult task was in part due to his own abilities, and in part to the assistance rendered him in this work by his chancellor, Thomas Becket, the clever young deacon whose talents had quickly won for him a leading place in Henry's counsels. We need not here relate in detail how Henry made him Archbishop of Canterbury against Becket's own wish, how they quarrelled over the Constitutions of Clarendon, and how their devoted friendship was turned to bitterest enmity.

Such was the state of affairs when, in 1164, the king resolved, by fair means or by foul, to effect the ruin of his one-time friend, whose unexpected opposition had baffled his plans to bring the Church courts under the royal control. Henry knew that, quite apart from his royal authority and the vigorous force of his own character, the position that he occupied was an extremely strong one. Becket could not look for much help from his old enemies, the barons ; the bishops were only lukewarm in his favour ; the pope was by no means likely to support him whole-heartedly.

So Becket was summoned to London by the king to answer for his alleged refusal to do justice to one John the Marshall. The archbishop pleaded illness and did not come. The king replied by calling together a council at Northampton to try Becket for his neglect of the royal summons. He was determined to bring charge after charge against the archbishop until he would be forced to resign his see.

The king took up his quarters at the Castle ; Becket, after some difficulty, managed to obtain shelter at the Priory of St. Andrew. The trial commenced on October 7th. A wearisome legal wrangle now began which lasted for several days. The king, his chief barons, and the bishops seem to have sat in an upper chamber, where the actual legal proceedings took place ; the sheriffs and lesser barons appear to have waited about in the Great Hall below.

First of all, the case of John the Marshall was decided. A long argument took place between the barons and the bishops as to which body ought to try the case. Each tried to thrust the responsibility on to the other. Finally, the king flew into a violent passion, and, as the chronicler tells us "the discussion was immediately ended." Discussions usually were "immediately ended" when Henry lost his temper. Henry, Bishop of Winchester, a brother of the late King Stephen, was then dispatched to inform Becket that judgment had been given against him, and that he must pay a fine of £500.

The king's wrath was not yet appeased ; he next called upon Becket to give an account of various sums of money, that had passed through his hands as chancellor.

The archbishop, whose health was giving way under the continued strain of his trial, protested against this, but in vain. Finally Henry demanded a full and detailed statement of what had become of every penny that Becket had received during the whole time he had held the chancellorship. Such a demand was obviously unreasonable. Becket had been released from all responsibility for his proceedings as chancellor when he had resigned that office after his consecration as archbishop. He had received no warning that such an account would be required of him at Northampton; it was impossible for him to state off-hand exactly how he had dealt with the £30,000 that had passed through his hands during the eight years he had held office. Nevertheless, the king refused to listen to any pleas for delay; he swore, with terrible oaths, that he would insist on seeing the full accounts in two days time. It was now clear that nothing but the complete ruin of his former friend would satisfy the enraged monarch.

In his perplexity, the primate, weak from bodily illness and mental exhaustion, sought counsel of the bishops at St. Andrew's Not much help came from them; few of them liked Thomas, and all of them were terribly afraid of the king. Gilbert Foliot, the Bishop of London, an old enemy of Becket, who was far from sorry to see the archbishop in such a position, counselled complete submission. "Remember from what a low estate the king raised you," said he. "Give up your archbishopric and humble yourself, perchance the king may forgive you if he sees you submissive."

Henry of Winchester, though he counselled prudence, feared what the result might be if Becket were forced to resign. There would then be no law in England but the king's will.

Hilary of Chichester, in a speech described as "gloriosus in verbis" by the chronicler, put the facts of the case plainly and truly enough. "You made many enemies when you were chancellor, because you served the king faithfully. The king, urged on by those enemies, now seeks to destroy you. What can you do but submit? Who dares to stand by you?"

The Bishop of Lincoln, whom the chronicler describes as "a simple man and of little discretion," argued as follows: "It is plain that this man must yield up either his archbishopric or his life, but what should be the use of the archbishopric to him if his life cease, I see not."

Finally Becket decided to offer to pay the king 2,000 marks (£1,333 6s. 8d.), although he declined to admit that he ought in justice to pay anything at all. This offer was scornfully refused. Becket, whose illness now confined him to the Priory, managed to obtain a grudging respite until Tuesday, October 13th. It was hinted that, if he did not give full satisfaction then, his life would be in danger.

The events of this fateful day have been variously reported and it is sometimes hard to reconcile the conflicting accounts of what happened. Becket, though still weak and ill, rose very early on Tuesday morning. The bishops, who seemed now to have lost what little courage they had ever possessed, flocked round him and tearfully besought him to yield. Thomas rebuked them for their cowardice, told them to refuse to take any further part in his trial, and to excommunicate any layman who dared to sit in judgment against him. He then announced his intention of appealing to Rome.

Next the archbishop donned his full robes of office and went into the Priory Church. Here he celebrated the Mass of St. Stephen, the first Christian martyr, by which he showed that he thought that his resistance to the king would cost him his life. Commending himself to the care of St. Stephen and of St. Elphege, the Saxon archbishop whom Sweyn's Northmen had murdered, Thomas left the church. His horse awaited him without. Still in his episcopal robes, and with his great cross borne before him, he rode out of the Priory gates. Only two of his attendants dared to follow him, for all men thought that he was going to his death. A great crowd of the citizens of Northampton awaited him; they had come out to show that, whatever king, barons, and bishops might think, the common people believed that Becket had right on his side.

Picture to yourself this remarkable scene; the cold dawn of an October day, the narrow street with its quaint wooden houses, the huge round mass of St. Sepulchre's overlooking all, the throngs of excited people, jostling and pushing one another to get near enough to the archbishop to ask his blessing, and, in the midst of it all, Thomas, his pale face firmly set and his eyes shining with a strange and unnatural light, as he rides on, clad in his gleaming vestments, following the great cross towards the Castle, where he deems that martyrdom awaits him. The streets we know so well have witnessed many a dramatic scene in the ages that have passed, but none more striking than this.

The appearance of Becket at the Great Gate in such a garb took everybody by surprise. Henry, when the news reached him, hurried away to the upper chamber with his chief barons to decide what was to be done. From beginning to end of the scene that followed he never stood face to face with Becket.

Taking the cross from the attendant who bore it, the archbishop passed slowly up the crowded Great Hall. The bishops, at first almost dumb with amazement, now came towards him and implored him to lay down the cross. They feared his action would provoke violence; Becket trusted that it might prevent it. "Were the king now to draw his sword," they argued, "archbishop and king would be fairly matched." "That we will commit to God," replied Thomas, turning from them to go to his usual place. Foliot, bitter as ever, snarled angrily, "A fool he ever was, and a fool he ever will be."

Then came a messenger from the king to summon the bishops to the chamber above. One by one they passed out through the door and up the stairway. Becket was left alone among the hostile courtiers.

Meanwhile, in the room above, the bishops were telling the king what had taken place at St. Andrew's, how Becket had commanded them to take no further part in the trial, and how he had appealed to Rome. They dared not sit in judgment on their superior, they said, in the face of this prohibition. Henry sent down an angry message, bidding Becket withdraw his appeal and submit to the judgment of the court. Thomas replied with a firm refusal. As the messenger withdrew, an ominous murmur ran round the crowded hall, that Henry's father had known how to deal with rebellious priests.

When Henry received Becket's reply his wrath knew no bounds. He at once called upon his council to judge the archbishop for his contempt of the king's court. Again the bishops pleaded their inability to pronounce judgment upon their superior. Henry turned upon them in a fury; they besought him to let them go, they would themselves appeal to Rome against the archbishop. Thus they escaped the responsibility of giving a decision, and, trembling in every limb, they made their way down the stairs again. "You have placed us between the hammer and the anvil," said Hilary of Chichester to Thomas. "What else could we do?"

Yet again a messenger came down, this time to command some of the more elderly sheriffs and barons to join the council upstairs. Overawed by the angry king, the council then condemned the archbishop as a traitor. Robert of Leicester, the aged justiciar, was ordered to pronounce the sentence, and, accompanied by some of the others, he went down to the Great Hall to fulfil his unpleasant task. All eyes turned upon the two men as they faced one another, the justiciar on the point of shedding tears, Becket, white and anxious, but still resolute.

The earl began to speak, but hardly a word had passed his lips when Thomas stopped him, crying aloud: "Who are ye that ye should judge me? Ye are but princes of the palace, lay persons! I am your spiritual father, and by my authority I forbid you to pronounce the sentence!" They fell back before him; Thomas, raising his cross aloft, turned to leave the hall. A sullen murmur ran through the ranks of his foes; it rose louder and louder. "Traitor!" cried someone, and, like a thunder burst, a roar of, "Traitor! Perjured traitor!" resounded through the room. Some snatched up faggots and rushes to cast at the primate; all joined in the savage outcry against him. Thomas swung round, his eyes blazing with wrath, and faced the leader of the angry throng. "Were I a knight instead of a priest," he cried, "this hand should show thee whether I were perjured or a traitor!" With that, he passed through the hostile ranks and out of the Great Hall. The door had been locked, but his attendant had found the key and opened it. Becket, unmolested, left the Castle and passed into the crowded streets. Here he was among friends. The people of Northampton, who had heard with the utmost fear the savage cries of Becket's foes, rejoiced to see him safe.

All the road to the Priory was lined with kneeling forms, and Becket, raising his hand in blessing as he passed, slowly made his way back to St. Andrew's. That night he shared his supper with the poor who waited about the gates, and at length he retired to sleep in the Priory Church, whither his bed had been moved at his request.

When morning broke again, Becket was gone. Realising the imminent danger of his position, he had ridden out secretly at midnight, dressed as a monk. With three companions he had slipped unnoticed through the North Gate, amid a heavy thunderstorm and pelting shower of rain that had deadened the sound of their horses' hoofs. By daybreak he was well on his way to the coast, whence he sailed for France.

A local tradition says that in his flight he drank from the well near Cheyne Walk that bears his name. This is extremely unlikely, as his road lay in a totally different direction. The structure above the well is quite modern.

What need to tell again the story of Becket's return, of the hasty words of Henry, and of the cruel murder in the cathedral that made the archbishop known to future generations as St. Thomas, the Martyr of Canterbury ?

CHAPTER X.

THE LAST OF THE SENLIS FAMILY.

THE murder of Thomas Becket in 1170 made Henry II. very unpopular in England and was one of the many causes which helped to bring about an event that had been threatening for some time. For years the barons had watched with dismay the growth of Henry's power ; they had begun to realise that never again would they be allowed to act as petty independent princes. Yet rebellion seemed to be out of the question ; the king's reforms, though distasteful to the baronage, had benefited the country. The common people, who greatly preferred the strong rule of Henry to the state of anarchy that had existed under Stephen, would be ready enough to support the king against any attempt to re-assert the power of the nobility. So the barons, though they saw their old local independence slipping away from them, were yet compelled to wait until some chance event lessened the king's popularity and made a successful revolt possible.

At last the murder of Becket gave them their opportunity. This terrible crime filled the heart of every Englishman with horror and indignation. Louis VII., who was anxious to recover the vast territories under Henry's influence in France, took advantage of the English king's temporary unpopularity and fomented the discontent in his rival's country. The barons in Henry's French possessions were ripe for revolt. His sons were ready to join the enemies of their own father. William the Lion, King of Scotland, was prepared to aid the rebels. Now or never was the barons' chance to free themselves from the domination of the crown.

Thus, in 1173, the last great feudal revolt broke out. Once and for ever, it was to be settled whether England was to be a strong, united kingdom, with a powerful central government and one great system of law, or a collection of practically independent baronies.

In the war that followed, a wide-spread war that raged throughout all Henry's dominions, from bleak Northumberland to sunny Gascony, Northampton took the king's side. Elsewhere may be read how the unconquerable resolution and marvellous energy of Henry broke down the opposition of those leagued against him; here we must follow the course of the war in Northamptonshire.

At Leicester, some forty miles away, lay the forces of Malory, the constable of that town, one of the rebel leaders. Malory resolved to attack our town, and in May, 1174, he appeared before the North Gate with a large army. If only the citizens had kept behind their strong line of walls, all would have been well. Unfortunately, being either over-confident of their strength, or angered by the taunts and jeers of the enemy, the burgesses made a sortie and attacked the rebel host. The result was disastrous; 200 of the townsmen were slain, almost as many were captured, and the remainder were glad to escape to the shelter of their fortifications, which they ought never to have left. The victorious rebels marched back to Leicester in triumph, a long train of prisoners following in their wake.

Yet, though the barons had the better of the affairs in this locality, their triumph was short-lived. By July, the rebellion was over. Henry, whose penance at the tomb of Becket had restored him to popular favour, was once more supreme in the land. On every side his enemies were laying down their arms and praying for pardon. At Northampton Henry received the surrender of the leaders of the late rebellion.

Here, too, he met William the Lion, a prisoner in the Castle. The unfortunate Scottish king, who was a grandson of Prince David and of Waltheof's daughter Matilda, had been captured at Alnwick on the very night of Henry's penance at Canterbury. The captive monarch, tied beneath the body of a horse, had been brought to Northampton Castle a few days later. In this ignominious manner, Waltheof's descendant passed through the streets of the town of which his great-grandfather had been the first earl.

Simon de Senlis III., the second cousin of the unfortunate Scottish king, was probably a witness of his relative's disgrace. If so, it is doubtful whether he felt much sympathy with the prisoner ; there had been a long-standing feud between them over the Earldom of Huntingdon, to which both had laid claim. Simon had fought on the king's side against the rebels in France, where he had been captured in 1173. By June, 1174, he had regained his freedom, and was besieging the town of Huntingdon. Henry II. promised to give him the earldom if he captured the town. Huntingdon was taken in July, and Simon de Senlis III. received the title that had been promised him.

Simon de Senlis III. inherited the family zeal for building, and it was he who rebuilt St. Peter's Church in late Norman style. The rounded arches that line the nave give us an idea of the shape of those that once surmounted the Norman pillars of St. Sepulchre's. It is probable that the arches in St. Sepulchre's were less elaborately ornamented than those of St. Peter's. When one examines the splendid examples of Norman work to be found in the latter church, it seems hard to believe that, in later years, some persons covered the whole of the beautiful structure with a mixture of plaster and white-wash. Yet such is the case ; we owe its restoration to the devotion and care of a lady, who, some sixty years ago, herself scraped away the ugly coating, using a bone knife blade lest steel should injure the fine work that lay concealed beneath.

It is not quite clear to what extent Simon de Senlis III. exercised authority in this town. He did not possess as much power here as did the first earl, but he was undoubtedly much more closely connected with the town from which he derived his title than is the modern Marquis of Northampton. There is no evidence to show that he was in any way oppressive or unjust, but it can hardly be doubted that the citizens were beginning to think that it was time they were allowed to manage their own affairs.

It must not be forgotten that at this period there was another person whose character was almost as important to the Northampton townspeople as that of their earl. This was the sheriff. It will be remembered that on every manorial estate there was a "reeve," a villein whose duty it was to see that his fellow-workers on the manor did their appointed tasks. Similarly, in every county, there was a "shire-reeve," or sheriff, who had to see that the inhabitants rendered the king what was due to him. In fact, the sheriff was an official appointed to watch over the royal interests in every way. There is still a sheriff appointed for Northamptonshire every year, but in these days his duties are not very arduous. The sheriff is still a very important person in some of the Western States of America.

Among the numerous duties of the Northamptonshire sheriff in early times, was that of collecting the *firma* of our town. The *firma* was the amount that the citizens had to pay to the king every year. In the reign of Henry II. this was £100.

Of course, the sheriff often had to spend money on the king's behalf. He took these sums from what he had collected, and paid over the remainder of the £100 to the Exchequer. In order that the king might not be cheated, the Exchequer officials made the sheriff give a full account of how and why he had spent money. We still possess copies of the sheriff's accounts. It will give us a glimpse of the life of the time if we examine a specimen of them. We will take as our example the accounts rendered of the *firma* of Northampton in 1176.

"Hugh de Gundeville renders account of £100 for the *firma* of the Borough of Northampton.

In the Treasury £96 0s. 5d.

And in alms paid to the Knights of the Temple in the Borough of Northampton one mark.

And to the monks of the same town 20s.

And to Hugh the son of Robert the son of Sawin 20s. in the meadow of Chingeshala.

And in the payments of John the clerk of Eleanor Queen of Spain who abode in the schools at Northampton 6s. for three weeks by the King's writ.

And to Hugh Saloman 12s. for the armour which he conveyed from Huntingdon to Northampton by the King's writ.

And for conveying treasure to Woodstock to Geddington and to London 7s. by Waleran and Odo de Fawsley.

And for executing justice upon William de Helford 15d.

And he is quit.

Let us look into this account. Hugh de Gundeville was the sheriff. He has paid in £96 0s. 5d., and he has to explain what he has done with the rest.

First of all there are the regular gifts of the king to two religious bodies; a mark (13s. 4d.) to the Knights of the Temple and £1 to the monks of St. Andrew's. These items occur in the account of the sheriff every year.

The payment in connection with the meadow of Chingeshala, the site of which we do not know, is another annual item. Robert, the son of Sawin, had been sheriff before Hugh de Gundeville. The king seems to have paid the late sheriff's son rent for the use of the meadow.

It will be seen from this entry how very awkward it was when surnames were not general; at the same time it shows how some modern surnames arose. It would have been much more simple to speak of Hugh, Robert's son, and for all Hugh's descendants to keep the same name Robertson, instead of having to write out a sort of table of descent after their Christian names every time. In course of time many people adopted this plan, hence the numerous Thomsons, Jacksons, Wilsons, Harrisons, Dixons, Watsons, Jamesons, and Robinsons of to-day.

John the clerk was an attendant of Eleanor, daughter of Henry II., who had been married to the King of Spain. Anybody who could read and write was then called a clerk. Eleanor was evidently on a visit to England, and, during her stay in Northampton, her clerk was accommodated at the "Schools" here, by the king's order.

It would be extremely interesting if we could find out a little more about these early "Schools." They were probably managed by the monks of St. Andrew's Priory. In the reign of Henry III. the "Schools" are again mentioned, one John of Duston, the vicar of a Northampton Church, being sent there for a year's tuition.

The sheriff has also spent a certain amount of money in conveying armour and treasure about the country. It may be noticed that Hugh Saloman has already discovered the advantages of a surname.

We do not know what happened to poor William de Helford, but probably it was something extremely unpleasant. What passed for "justice" in the Middle Ages would be considered barbarous cruelty to-day.

If these items are added up it will be seen that they come to exactly £3 19s. 7d. The sheriff has already paid in £96 0s. 5d., so "he is quit," that is, he has accounted for the £100 due from him to the satisfaction of the Exchequer officials.

We know nothing about the personal character of Hugh de Gundeville, but, if he was like the majority of the sheriffs of that time, he probably extorted a good deal more than £100 from the Northampton burgesses and kept the balance himself. Moreover, he doubtless interfered with the liberty of the citizens in countless small matters. Northampton was now an important place, and its inhabitants were beginning to resent the domination of the sheriff. How much better it would be, thought the burgesses, if we could get a charter from the king as the people of Oxford and London have done. Then we could collect the *firma* and pay it over ourselves, we could elect one of our leading townsmen to be our ruler, and we should be free from all outside interference.

In 1185, Simon de Senlis III. died. He was the last of his line, for, although he had had a son, the boy's death had taken place some years previously. The Senlis family was extinct.

Perhaps the earl had viewed with displeasure any attempts made by the citizens during his lifetime to improve their position. At all events, his death coincided with a step forward towards municipal independence. Immediately after the death of Simon, the burgesses applied to Henry II. for permission to hold the town of him *in capite*, that is to say, they desired to be allowed to collect the *firma* themselves and to hand it over in a lump sum. Thus they would escape the exactions of the sheriff.

Henry II., who had been a frequent visitor to Northampton during the years that had followed the suppression of the last great feudal rebellion, granted their request. They had to pay for the privilege the sum of 200 marks, and in addition the yearly *firma* was increased to £120.

The burgesses paid the money cheerfully. The benefits obtained far outweighed the extra expenditure; indeed, quite apart from other advantages, it is probable that a great deal more than the extra £20 had found its way into the pockets of the sheriff every year. Now Northampton was dependent upon the king and upon the king alone. The Senlis family had done great things for the town, but, after all, they had been alien rulers imposed upon the inhabitants by a foreign conqueror. Now Northampton, free from the control of the sheriff and earl alike, was well on its way to obtaining the charter that, early in the next reign, was to gain for our town complete municipal freedom.*

* NOTE TO CHAPTER X. Although no town charter earlier than that of 1189 is extant, some authorities consider that the change made in tenure in 1185 must have involved the grant of some kind of charter. After a careful study of the evidence for and against this view, I have decided to assume that the first charter was granted in 1189. The existence of an earlier one is, to say the least of it, highly problematical.

CHAPTER XI.

NORTHAMPTON GAINS ITS CHARTER.

RICHARD I. ascended the throne at a time when all Europe was astir with religious zeal and military preparation. Two years previous to the death of Henry II., Jerusalem, which had been in the Crusaders' hands for nearly ninety years, had once more been captured by the Saracens. Now, in every Christian country, men were being mustered and armed, thousands of gallant knights were taking the cross, rival kings were swearing to abandon their quarrels and to fight side by side for the cause of Christendom. A great international army was about to set forth for Palestine to make another attempt to wrest the Holy City from the iron grip of Saladin.

Foremost among the monarchs who had vowed their lives to the Crusade was the brave and chivalrous Richard. He had resolved to take with him to Palestine a force that should excel in splendour every other army in the great Crusading host. To do this, much money was needed, far more than the royal treasury could supply. Richard intended to raise this money by every means in his power.

The Northampton burgesses were no doubt as enthusiastic about the Crusade as the inhabitants of any other English town. As they knelt in worship at St. Sepulchre's, the citizens must have thought of the famous church of the same name at Jerusalem, that was now in the hands of the infidel, and must have prayed fervently for the success of the Crusaders Probably the ranks of Richard's army contained some sturdy Northamptonians, ready to fight, and, if need be, to die in the cause of the Cross.

Yet, while this spirit of religious zeal was sweeping over the land, there were other burgesses, who realised that the king's necessity was Northampton's opportunity. Richard wanted money; he would give anything to get money; he had already sold privileges, honours and offices of all kinds for money. Now was the time to obtain the long-desired charter.

Exactly what bargain was made we do not know; probably a considerable sum of money passed from the hands of the burgesses to those of Richard's treasurers. At all events, on November 18th, 1189, Northampton received its charter from the king.

This document, which is still kept among the borough records, is a yellow piece of parchment about 16 inches wide and 6½ inches deep, covered with the curious abbreviated Latin used at that period. It is interesting to us to-day as a relic of old Northampton; to our ancestors it was precious beyond all price as the document to which they owed their freedom from the exactions which they begrudged, their exemption from customs which they hated, and the right to govern themselves, which had been their ambition for so many years.

The following were the chief privileges granted by the charter.

1.—The burgesses were to elect a reeve every year, who should govern the town, and collect the *firma* of £120, which he would then pay over to the king.

2.—Every week, the reeve was to hold a court of justice in the town. No Northampton burgess was to be tried outside his own town, except in certain specified cases.

3.—The customs of the borough concerning landholding and debt should be observed as law in the town.

4.—No Northampton burgess should be forced to accept a challenge to trial by battle.

5.—No fine need be paid by the town if the body of an unknown murdered man was found there.

6.—No Northampton burgess should be compelled by the king's marshall to provide board and lodging to the king's followers without payment.

7.—Northampton burgesses were to be free from the tolls and payments imposed upon strangers by other towns.

If anyone in another town exacted such tolls or payments from Northampton burgesses, the reeve of Northampton might retaliate by seizing the goods of any merchants from that town who came here.

Such were the principal provisions of the charter of 1189. It was not long before the title given to the chief citizen of the town was changed. After about 1250 we hear no more of the reeve ; he is henceforth always spoken of as the mayor.

The reeve was elected by a general assembly of the burgesses, who gathered together annually for this purpose in some large open space. In later years St. Giles' Churchyard, or the nave of the church itself, was the scene of this annual election, and perhaps such was the case from the very beginning Some think, however, that in early days the general assembly met on the Chequers, a piece of waste ground that lay where the Market Square is now.

It was not until many years later that the Chequers became the central square of the town. Northampton, being originally a river-side settlement, and being bounded by the Nene on the south and west, has expanded mainly in a north-easterly direction. In the 12th century, when it was still a comparatively small town, its central square was not the Chequers but the Mayorhold. Perhaps it was in the Mayorhold that the general assembly was first held.

Around the Mayorhold were all the principal streets of the town. The first town-hall was built in Scarletwell Street, a thoroughfare which derived its name from a celebrated well situated at its western extremity. This well was very famous in mediæval times ; its waters were supposed to be especially suited for use in process of dyeing garments, an industry which flourished greatly in that part of Northampton. Of the other thoroughfares near the Mayorhold, Sheep Street and the Horsemarket still recall by their names the time when sheep and cattle were bought and sold in the principal streets. Another street in this locality, which is known as Bath Street, was then called Hogmarket Lane. The name of the Mayorhold itself has a similar origin ; it was not so called because the mayor once performed his official duties near that spot.

In mediæval times it was called the Marehold, the square where mares were sold on market days. The present spelling is comparatively modern, as is the application of the name Marefair to the western part of Gold Street.

The mention of Gold Street should remind us of the existence in mediæval Northampton of a Jewry, or Jews' quarter. Silver Street (which then included College Street) and Gold Street were both inhabited by these alien money-lenders.

The position of the Jews in mediæval England was a curious one. At first sight it seems strange that they were allowed to live in this country at all, when one considers the bitter prejudice against them, both as foreigners and as the race that had rejected Christianity and persecuted the early Christians. Had their treatment depended solely upon the attitude of the barons, the clergy, and the common people towards them, they would soon have been exterminated or driven from the country.

There was, however another factor to be considered, and that was the attitude of the king. Mediæval kings frequently wanted to borrow money, and, as it was then considered a sin for a Christian to lend money on interest, no class of Christian moneylenders existed. The Jews, on the other hand, who were not allowed to compete with Christians in ordinary trade, took to moneylending as the one occupation open to them. Thus they were very useful to the king, who protected them from popular indignation and allowed them to exact interest from his subjects, in order that he himself might be able to draw upon the Jews' hoards in time of necessity.

It must not be imagined, however, that they were allowed to live in conditions of equality with the Christians. No king would have been strong enough to enforce such a state of affairs. The Jews had to keep to their own quarters and to wear a distinctive dress. Every Good Friday our worthy ancestors drove them to church in a body, where they were compelled to listen to an abusive sermon directed against the sins of their race. By this annual method of relieving their outraged Christian sensibilities, and by occasionally beating an unfortunate Jew to death, the Northampton burgesses quieted any qualms of conscience they may have felt for their sin in allowing such a detestable race to exist in a Christian country.

Elsewhere, however, the hatred of the populace for the Jews was not so easily appeased. The coronation of Richard was the signal for a general outburst of violence against the detested aliens. Hundreds of Jews were murdered and an immense amount of booty was stolen. Although the presence of a royal garrison in the Castle, and the fact that the townspeople were on their best behaviour, because of their recently acquired charter, prevented any anti-Jewish riots in this town, the disturbance elsewhere led to the occurrence at Northampton of an incident which shows us at once the worst and best aspects of the mediæval Church.

Stamford was one of the towns in which the Jews had been robbed and murdered. One of the rioters, John of Stamford, had stolen a large sum of money during the plunder of the Jewry there. Fearing that his ill-gotten gains would be confiscated by the king's officers, he fled to Northampton, and took refuge in the house of an undesirable character who dwelt in this town. This man soon turned his greedy eyes towards the stolen riches of his visitor. We know nothing of the details of the black crime that followed; let it suffice that one morning John's dead body was found outside the walls, and that his host fled from the town, bearing with him the treasure that had cost the Stamford rioter his life.

Plain as it would seem that John of Stamford had been murdered by the missing man, rumour now began to connect the Jews with the crime. The story grew as it passed from mouth to mouth; John of Stamford had been murdered by the Jews; John of Stamford had died a martyr for the Christian Church; miracles had been performed at John of Stamford's tomb; John of Stamford was the greatest saint of the age. Before long, visitors were flocking in from all the neighbouring villages and towns to worship at the shrine of that blessed martyr, St. John of Stamford, and the dead thief's burial place in All Saints' Church was thickly covered with votive offerings.

The rapidly growing legend was encouraged by the Northampton clergy and also by some of the burgesses, who anticipated a golden harvest if this town became a centre for pilgrims. But if the local clergy imagined that they would be allowed to perpetrate a fraud of this kind for the sake of gain, they reckoned without their bishop.

Hugh, Bishop of Lincoln, a diocese that then included Northampton, was one of those saintly men whose lives, shining all the more brightly amid the surrounding darkness, light up the gloomy pages of mediæval history. He was not the man to permit such an imposture to continue. Hastening to Northampton, he gave peremptory orders that this attempt to glorify the memory of a criminal should cease. This action caused a violent outburst of popular feeling. A crowd of burgesses, many of them armed, burst into the church and threatened vengeance upon any who should interfere with the tomb of the supposed martyr. The bishop did not flinch. Boldly he stood forth, and denounced the greed and impiety of those who had attempted to impose upon the simplicity of their fellow Christians. His words prevailed. The citizens shrank abashed from the angry prelate, and Hugh, tearing down the votive offerings with his own hand, threatened to excommunicate any person who should worship at the tomb in future. After this we hear no more of the Stamford martyr.

Little else of importance took place in Northampton during the reign of Richard. The king held one Great Council here after his return from captivity. and we may imagine the burgesses warmly welcoming the author of their municipal independence, albeit their ardour must have been a little cooled by the thought of the amount they had just been obliged to contribute towards his ransom. Richard's reign marks the beginning of a new epoch in Northampton's story. Material prosperity had been attained under the domination of a Norman earl, but not until the charter won civic freedom for Northampton, was it possible for the corporate life of our town to be developed to its fullest extent.

NORTHAMPTON CASTLE. (The Postern Gate—Interior).

Reproduced from The Rev. R. M. Serjeantson's "Castle of Northampton," by permission of the Author, and the Northants. Natural History Society.

CHAPTER XII.

KING JOHN.

THE monarch whose name gives this chapter its title is generally considered to have been the worst man that ever sat upon the English throne. His reign is one long record of quarrels, quarrels with his overlord, Philip of France, quarrels with the Church, quarrels with the Londoners, quarrels with the baronage, quarrels with the whole nation. Several incidents connected with these various disputes took place in our town, for the one redeeming feature of John's character seems to have been his liking for Northampton. During the seventeen years of his reign we have records of no less than thirty visits to this town. It is worth noticing that Shakespeare's play, "King John," contains several scenes that are supposed to take place at Northampton.

When Richard I. died, John, who was then in Normandy, at once claimed the throne. Many people, however, looked upon John's nephew Arthur as the rightful heir, so the new king sent over Hubert Walter, the Archbishop of Canterbury, and William Marshall, the old Earl of Pembroke, to secure England for him, while he fought against Arthur's adherents in France. A Great Council was summoned to Northampton by these two representatives of the king, and here all those barons whose loyalty was suspected were compelled to swear allegiance to John.

Shakespeare in his play represents the death of Arthur as having been caused by a fall from the walls of Northampton Castle, while attempting to escape from captivity in that fortress. There is no authority for this tale. Shakespeare was a dramatist, not a historian; his aim was to write a good play, not to keep within the narrow bounds of historical truth.

Having contrived to lose Normandy by quarrelling with Philip, John next fell out with the Londoners. The result of this quarrel was the removal of the king's treasury to Northampton for some months.

The king's residence at Northampton was not wholly without advantage to the town. While here, he frequently disobeyed the law of the Church by eating meat and drinking wine on fast days. Sometimes, when he had indulged in a particularly heavy orgy, his conscience troubled him the next morning, and he was wont to quiet it by giving alms to the poor of the town. On one occasion, no less than 1,000 were fed at his expense, each being supplied with beer, bread, and and fish or meat. John's act of charity cost him £5 14s. 7d., which gives us some idea of the purchasing power of money at that time.

In 1208, when England was under an interdict, the pope sent the legate Pandulf to England to try to induce John to yield to the papal authority and to accept Stephen Langton as archbishop. Pandulf came to Northampton and met John in the Great Hall, which had formerly been the scene of Becket's defiance of the royal authority. Here John, surrounded by his barons, received the message of the papal legate.

A heated argument took place, the king persistently declining to allow Langton to return to England as archbishop, though he offered some concessions to the demands of the legate. Finally Pandulf announced that John was excommunicated and deposed from his throne and in the name of the pope released the king's subjects from their allegiance.

John replied in a striking manner. The pope had taken his kingly authority from him! Had he? Pandulf should see that the king's power was still as great as ever. Calling for certain prisoners to be brought before him, he began to order various punishments to be inflicted upon them. One he sentenced to be hanged, he told his servants to blind another, a third was condemned to have his hands and feet struck off. As each unhappy wretch was dragged out to his doom, John looked towards the legate to see what effect this display of royal authority would have upon him. Pandulf knew not whether the next order might not be for his own death, but he remained calm and unmoved. At last John, resolved to shake the courage of the undaunted legate, cried, "Bring forth that rascal priest, that justice may be done upon him."

A man standing among the miserable group of prisoners was seized and roughly thrust before the king. He was a priest, who had been charged with some crime. With an evil smile wreathing his face, the king, still glancing in the direction of the legate, said: "Take him hence and hang him." The gaolers prepared to drag the luckless priest from the hall, but, ere they could achieve their purpose, Pandulf, roused from his calm at last, stepped forward and spoke. "None but a priest may judge a priest. Unhand that clerk, or you, too, will be excommunicated." Those who held the prisoner hesitated, their fear of the king combating with their fear of the Church. Pandulf prepared to carry out his threat, and, not having with him the candle necessary for the ceremony of excommunication, he calmly left the hall to find one.

For a moment John sat amazed, then came one of those swift changes from boldness to craven fear which were so common with him. Springing from his seat, he ran down the hall after the legate and besought him not to excommunicate his servants. He would hand over the priest to be judged by Pandulf himself. The legate thereupon went back to the hall and pronounced the freedom of the condemned man.

Such was the power of the Church in mediæval times.

Pandulf's interview with John did not lead to a settlement of the quarrel with the pope, and it was not until two years later that the king yielded and consented to receive Langton. No sooner was the conflict with the Church ended than that with the baronage began. After years of bickering, matters came to a head in 1215, when the nobility, disgusted by the alternate tyranny and cowardice of the king, resolved to enforce better government by rising in arms against him.

The citizens of Northampton were opposed to the king, though the Castle, which was held by John's mercenaries, remained loyal to him. When war broke out, a great baronial army, under the leadership of Robert Fitz-Walter, marched from Brackley to Northampton, and, being admitted to the town by the burgesses, besieged the Castle. It was a hard matter in those times to capture a strong fortress like Northampton Castle, even if the besiegers were fully equipped with siege appliances and engines of war, which the barons were not. Hence their only hope lay in the possibility of the garrison being short of provisions. Such, however, did not prove to be the case, and, after about a fortnight, the barons abandoned the siege as hopeless and marched away to Bedford. Little loss of life had been sustained by either party, the only man slain being Fitz-Walter's standard bearer, who was shot dead by a cross-bowman of the garrison.

Some weeks later the Northampton burgesses themselves seem to have made an attempt to attack the Castle. Apparently they took the defenders by surprise, for it is stated that several of the garrison were killed. In revenge, the mercenaries made a sortie and succeeded in burning down part of the town.

These minor skirmishes did not affect the main issue. John had neither the men nor the money for a prolonged struggle. In June, 1215, he yielded to the barons' demands, and the Great Charter was signed at Runnymede.

The king had no intention of keeping the peace that had been thrust upon him. During the next three months he steadily prepared for a fresh war. Then civil strife again raged in England, and once more the baronial forces besieged Northampton Castle. This time they had with them French artificers who were skilled in the construction of siege engines. A determined assault was made upon the royal fortress, but John, marching rapidly to the rescue with a formidable army of Flemish mercenaries, came up in time to save the threatened stronghold, and again the barons were compelled to raise the siege.

John's sudden death in 1216 did not conclude the war, but by the end of the next year all was over. In 1218 the boy king, Henry III., kept Christmas at Northampton, where he was entertained by the Constable of the Castle, Fawkes de Breauté.

This baron, who had been one of the chief leaders of John's mercenaries, was destined to cause considerable trouble in later years. During the civil war he had managed to obtain possession of several of the royal castles, and he showed no inclination to give them up to the young king. For several years his excessive power was a menace to the peace of the realm, but at last he went too far and brought about his own ruin.

In 1224, Fawkes de Breauté was fined by a judge at Bedford for encroaching upon another man's land. He revenged himself upon the judge by ordering him to be seized and thrown into a dungeon in Bedford Castle. The wife of the unhappy prisoner fled to Northampton to seek redress from the king, who was just gathering his barons together for an expedition to France. On receipt of the news, a powerful force, nominally under the command of Henry, set out for Bedford. Fawkes de Breauté fled, but his brother William, who had carried out the actual seizure of the judge, held Bedford Castle against the royal troops. After a siege of two months the castle was surrendered. William de Breaute was taken prisoner and promptly hanged; his brother contrived to escape capture for some time. Finally he took sanctuary at Coventry, but was handed over to Stephen Langton and brought to Northampton to be tried. Although his former services to John saved his life, he was deprived of all his property and exiled.

It will be seen from this chapter that a great change had come over the baronage since the days of the last great feudal revolt. Then they had aimed at local independence and freedom from royal control, in John's reign they acted as a united body to prevent tyranny, whether the tyrant were a king or only an overpowerful captain of mercenaries. Though still actuated to some extent by selfish motives, they were becoming in a sense the leaders of the nation, not merely lawless foreign nobles ruling over a subject race. The loss of Normandy had made them think of England as their fatherland; till then, they could never quite rid themselves of the idea that it was a conquered province. This change was an excellent thing for England, but its effects upon the prosperity of Northampton were not so favourable, as will be seen later.

NORTHAMPTON CASTLE. (THE BASTION).

Reproduced from The Rev. R. M. SERJEANTSON's "Castle of Northampton," by permission of the Author, and the Northants. Natural History Society.

CHAPTER XIII.

MEDIÆVAL NORTHAMPTON.

DURING the forty years that followed the death of John, Northampton enjoyed complete freedom from the horrors of civil strife. This period was a time of steady progress and of development of the power of self-government gained by the charter of Richard I. This charter was renewed again and again by later kings, for at that time it was not yet clearly established that the reigning monarch was bound by the acts of his predecessors. Various new provisions were inserted from time to time, some of which we shall have occasion to notice hereafter. For example, John's charter to Northampton provided for the appointment of two bailiffs to assist the reeve in enforcing the customs of the town.

The reeve and his bailiffs made ample use of the powers entrusted to them. The most striking point to a modern observer about the regulations then in force in Northampton is the clearly marked distinction between burgesses and strangers. Like all other townsmen of this period, the Northampton burgesses regarded those who came from other parts of England as foreigners. Little encouragement was given to strangers who wished to do business in Northampton; the local merchants had no intention of allowing outside competitors to spoil their trade.

When we speak of merchants, we must remember that in the Middle Ages there was not the distinction between the manufacturer, the wholesale merchant, and the retail tradesman, that exists to-day. The Northampton merchant of the 13th century was generally a combination of all three. He manufactured his goods himself, sold them wholesale if he had a favourable offer made him, and, if not, was quite prepared to dispose of them retail.

In most towns an association of the merchants existed, and usually this merchant gild, as it was called, exercised a great deal of power in the choice of the town officials. To this day our chief municipal building is called the Guildhall. Naturally the reeve, who would always be a member of the merchant gild, framed all his regulations so as to benefit the town trade at the expense of strangers.

For example, if a wool-merchant from another district came into the town he was not allowed to start a retail business here. He might sell his wool wholesale and then depart, but he must sell it to a burgess; our ancestors did not allow strangers to outbid them in their own town.

Sometimes, of course, merchants arrived from other parts with goods that were not sold retail in the town, but which were necessary to local trades. Take, for example, the blue dye called woad. A stranger merchant might sell his woad retail to the dyers of Scarletwell Street, but he was not allowed to make profits in the town without paying for the privilege of doing so. For every quarter of woad that he sold he had to pay sixpence to the town bailiffs.

One of the most curious customs of the time was that concerning countrymen who brought in loads of straw to sell. They were not permitted to lower their burden from their head to the ground until they had sold it. If they violated this custom, the straw was promptly confiscated. The burgesses intended that the countrymen should sell their straw to the first would-be purchaser, not that they should stand about haggling over the price.

The burgesses took great care to protect themselves from any claims made by owners of manors to the effect that inhabitants of the town were escaped villeins. It was laid down that if any man had dwelt in Northampton for a year and a day, paying his share towards the town expenses, no lord had any right to question his freedom. This was a common law in mediæval towns.

Another custom made it unlawful for a burgess to lend money to a knight or any other person, if he had been informed by a fellow-burgess that the would-be borrower already owed money in the town . The penalty for breaking this rule was a fine of £2, a sum which would then be about equal to £40 in modern money.

It will be seen from the above examples that the reeve and his subordinates were people who wielded considerable power, at all events within their own town. There were, however, still two rival authorities whose position must have given them a certain amount of influence in Northampton affairs.

The first of these was the Constable of the Castle. Nominally, he had no right to exercise any authority in the town, but, as the direct representative of the king, he had no doubt tried frequently to encroach upon the privileges of the burgesses. The fight between the citizens and the garrison in John's reign seems to point to the existence of previous ill feeling.

The other authority was the Priory of St. Andrew, which exerted considerable influence, because of its control over all the Northampton churches. We have already noticed four of these, All Saints', St. Sepulchre's, St. Peter's, and St. Giles' ; there were in addition several others at the beginning of Henry III.'s reign, of which no trace now remains, though in several cases a modern church bearing the same name has been erected on or near the site of the mediæval building.

In the reign of John, some of the town churches showed signs of resenting the authority exercised over them by the French Priory of St. Andrew. They began to found chapels without first obtaining the consent of the prior, and in consequence an appeal was made to Rome by the monks. Innocent III., the pope with whom John quarrelled later, wrote to the Archbishop of Canterbury in 1201, ordering him to see that the exclusive privileges of the Priory were maintained.

A change that took place about this time was the abolition of the practice of holding a fair in All Saints' Church. This fair had been held regularly from a very early date, and was evidently a well established institution in the time of Simon de Senlis II., who granted a tenth of its profits to the Priory of St. Andrew. To us the idea of holding a fair in such a place seems extraordinary, but such practices were extremely common in the Middle Ages. It chanced, however, that in 1235 the Bishopric of Lincoln was in the hands of the famous Robert Grosstête, a man whose ideals were much loftier than those of his contemporaries. Grosstête prevailed upon Henry III. to prevent the fair from being held in the church. The king therefore issued a decree, in which he ordered it to be held in future " in the void and waste place on the north side of the church." This decree helped to make this " void and waste place " what it afterwards became—the Market Square.

Bishop Grosstête was the chief supporter of the friars, who first came to England in about 1224. As Northampton was one of the most important towns in his diocese, it is not surprising to learn that they came here in large numbers.

The Franciscans, or Grey Friars, established a small settlement here two years after they first appeared in this country. For a time they had their local headquarters in a small house near St. Giles' Church, but later, as their numbers increased, they built a large friary in Newland, on a piece of waste ground given them by the townsmen.

The Dominicans, or Black Friars, came to Northampton a few years after the Franciscans. Their friary was situated in the Horsemarket, not far from the Marehold. In later years two other orders came to the town, the Carmelites, or White Friars, taking up their abode in Newland, close to the Franciscan friary, and the Austin Friars settling in Kingswell Street.

Although, by the time of Chaucer, the friars had become notorious for their indolence and luxury, they were at first devout and unselfish men, who did excellent work, especially among the sick and the poor. Like their patron Grosstête, they took Simon de Montfort's side in his opposition to the Court, and their presence in the town may have helped to cause Northampton to give that great leader the support he received from our town during the eventful years that marked the close of the reign of Henry III.

CHAPTER XIV.

NORTHAMPTON A UNIVERSITY TOWN.

HENRY III. has been not inaptly described as the "waxen king." Although he was not without the strain of unreasoning obstinacy that is so often found in men of weak character, those who had once acquired an influence over him could mould him to whatever shape they chose. Throughout his reign, he allowed a horde of worthless and greedy foreign favourites to thrust themselves into the chief offices of church and state.

Under these circumstances, it is not to be wondered at that a national party arose in opposition to the alien courtiers upon whom the king had bestowed so many favours. The feeling between the two factions became ever more and more embittered. On three separate occasions, both sides were anxious to settle their differences by holding a tournament at Northampton, at which the English barons would joust against Henry's foreign friends. Each time this was suggested, Henry, fearing that the tournament would end in a desperate life and death struggle, prohibited the meeting. On the third occasion, the rival parties agreed to ignore the king's prohibition, and to hold the tournament in spite of him, but a deep fall of snow prevented them from carrying out their design.

A few years before Henry's continued misrule led to open war, an event took place, which might have changed the whole future history of our town. This was the migration of the Oxford and Cambridge scholars to Northampton.

The universities of the thirteenth century were very different in every respect from those of the present day. None of the magnificent college buildings, whose beauty now makes Oxford and Cambridge famous throughout the world, existed then. The students were scattered about those towns in various houses and taverns, no system of university discipline was maintained, and there were no courses of organized study. Some of the scholars were of noble birth, but the majority were extremely poor and did not hesitate to beg in the streets. They were all hot-blooded and high-spirited, and, when not engaged in combats with the townsfolk, they were in the habit of fighting among themselves, northerners versus southerners.

Despite their wild, lawless ways, they possessed a genuine zeal for knowledge. Much of their time was wasted in the study of a debased kind of logic; they would argue solemnly and at great length as to the number of spirits that could dance on the point of a needle. Yet, amid all the follies and perversions of mediæval learning, the universities produced some great thinkers and were a decided force in the life of the nation.

In 1238, a serious affray took place at Oxford between some of the students and the followers of the papal legate Otto. In consequence of this, many of the Oxford scholars migrated to Northampton. It was not until more than twenty years later that their presence here was authorised by the king. In 1258, by the Provisions of Oxford, Simon de Montfort and his supporters took the royal authority out of the hands of Henry III., and placed him under the control of a committee of barons. Three years later, the king, who was still controlled by this baronial committee, issued a decree permitting the establishment of a university at Northampton.

A year or two later there seem to have been several thousand scholars in our town, some from Cambridge, but most of them from Oxford. It is hard to say how the newcomers would have fared with the Northampton burgesses, had the settlement been a permanent one. However, as it happened, the University of Northampton was not destined to have a very lengthy existence.

Meanwhile Simon de Montfort was no longer on friendly terms with many of the barons who had joined him at first, and the king, emboldened by the dissensions among his enemies, refused to be bound by the Provisions of Oxford. The matter was referred to the arbitration of Louis IX., of France, who decided in Henry's favour, on the ground that the pope had absolved the English king from his oath. Simon de Montfort refused to accept the decision and prepared for open war.

Early in 1264, before hostilities had actually begun, Simon de Montfort the younger and Peter de Montfort, sons of the great earl, were sent to Northampton to secure the town for their father's cause. The Castle was already in the hands of one of their party, Ralph Basset. Northampton welcomed the young De Montforts, and, aided by the Castle garrison and by the newly arrived Oxford scholars, the burgesses prepared to offer a vigorous resistance to the royal forces, should any attempt be made to regain the town for the king.

They had not long to wait. Northampton and its castle were of such great importance that Henry's first thought was to recapture them. Early in April, the king and young Prince Edward arrived before the walls with a formidable army and commenced to lay siege to the town.

The defenders, confident in the strength of their walls, were not greatly perturbed by the advent of the Royalist army. They knew quite well that the king could not wait to starve them out, for Earl Simon himself had a force in the field, with which the besiegers would soon have to reckon. An assault upon the walls seemed out of the question. No doubt, if the Royalists once got into the town, their superiority in mail-clad knights would gain for them an easy victory, but, although the Oxford scholars would stand little chance against the charge of mail-clad horsemen in the open, they were all expert bowmen and slingers, and from the vantage of the walls they would probably be able to repel any storming party.

There was, however, one danger that the defenders of Northampton had overlooked. Though the inhabitants of town and Castle alike were staunch supporters of De Montfort's cause, the monks of St. Andrew's Priory were very much the reverse. To most men, Henry's liking for foreign priests was his worst fault; it was not to be expected that a community of French monks would see matters in the same light.

Henry was unpopular because he allowed the pope to exercise too much power in England ; this would not be resented by those who owed their continued supremacy over the Northampton churches to the intervention of Innocent III. So, although the monks had not openly opposed the reception of De Montfort's sons, they had already come to an understanding with the king's party.

On the second day of the siege, the defenders of the wall, who were ready to repel any assault that might be made upon the South Gate, before which the king's army was arrayed, saw a herald approaching under a flag of truce. Henry desired a parley, and he had sent to ask the leaders of the besieged force to meet him in the Cow Meadow to see whether a peaceful settlement could not be arranged.

On a previous occasion, when De Montfort's party had taken up arms, Henry had come to terms before any serious engagement had taken place. He was evidently about to do so again. The defenders at once prepared to commence negotiations, abandoning their vigilance and crowding eagerly to the southern walls to see what they could of the parley.

While the attention of all was diverted to the conference that was about to take place, the monks of St. Andrew's were carrying out the treachery they had planned. In secret, they had already partially undermined the portion of the town wall that adjoined the Priory garden, and now they hastened to complete their work. With a resounding crash the wall fell down. Instantly a body of forty picked horsemen, who had been lying in wait some distance off, galloped rapidly in towards the breach, young Prince Edward at their head.

The noise of the falling wall was heard all over the town, and, for the moment, the defenders were panic-stricken. Young Simon de Montfort and two of his friends alone seem to have kept their heads. The instant they heard the crash, they sprang on to their horses' backs and rode off at full speed through the streets in the direction of the Priory. Urging their chargers on with voice and spur, they burst into the Priory gardens just as the first few stormers were making their way through the breach. The three knights rode straight at them, and, after a few moments of desperate fighting, the Royalists were driven out in headlong confusion.

Everything depended upon the next few minutes. Could De Montfort and his friends but hold the breach till help arrived, all would be well. Again the attack surged on, again the stormers recoiled before the heavy blows of the three knights. Like his father, young Simon was a mighty warrior, and in the narrow breach the superior numbers of the assailants availed them nothing.

Determined to carry the breach before their opponents were reinforced, the Royalists were once again pressing on, when suddenly young Simon's steed plunged madly forward through the breach into the midst of his master's foes. De Montfort was thrown violently into the ditch by the furious animal, and in a moment a dozen swords were at his throat. He was forced to yield, and, disheartened by his capture, the remaining defenders were swept back by a determined rush. With a triumphant shout, the Royalist horsemen poured through the breach and galloped across the garden out into the streets.

Little further resistance was offered. The Oxford students made an attempt to check the enemy, but they were ridden down by the mail-clad knights. The Castle, in which a few of the defenders had taken refuge, held out, but on the next day it was so hotly assailed that it was surrendered. Peter de Montfort and Ralph Basset were captured, and many other knights with them, while the victorious army plundered the town, stripping the churches of their ornaments and the merchants' shops of their goods.

Henry III. entered Northampton in triumph and at first was disposed to deal very harshly with the Oxford scholars. Indeed, it is said that he intended to hang them all, for they had wrought much havoc among his troops with their bows and slings before they had been overpowered. Henry's barons protested warmly against such drastic measures; many of the youthful rebels were sons of the king's chief supporters, and, if he hanged them, their fathers would certainly change sides. Eventually Henry yielded to the arguments of his followers and spared the scholars' lives, but he determined to make an end of Northampton University. All the Oxford students were ordered to leave the town and never to return.

The rest of the war does not closely concern Northampton. After the battle of Lewes, the town again fell into the hands of De Montfort's party. When the great earl was defeated and slain at Evesham, Northampton at once threw open its gates to the royal forces.

This prompt submission seems to have restored the town to royal favour. A general pardon was issued to all who had taken part in the recent rebellion, and, during the remainder of his reign, Henry III., like so many of his predecessors, spent a great deal of his time here.

An incident of considerable importance took place at Northampton towards the end of the reign. In 1268, Prince Edward, with a number of other knights, came here to take the cross, before setting out upon the crusade from which he was destined to return as King of England. The papal legate, Ottoboni, preached such a stirring sermon on this occasion that the townsfolk rushed forward in large numbers, desiring to follow the prince upon his expedition.

Among those present when Edward took the cross was his wife, the beautiful Eleanor of Castile. She accompanied her husband to Palestine and shared with him the hardships and dangers of the Crusade. Afterwards Eleanor returned safely home and for nearly twenty years was Queen of England. When she died at Harby, in Nottinghamshire, in 1290, her sorrowing husband caused crosses to be erected near each place where her embalmed body had rested for the night on its way to London. The corpse rested at De la Pré Abbey on the night that the funeral procession halted at our town, and the remains of the cross stand just outside the grounds of the nunnery. The top of the monument is gone, and time has left its mark upon the remainder, but still it stands by the roadside, a lasting memorial of the love and devotion of the greatest of the Plantagenets.

CHAPTER XV.

NORTHAMPTON AT ITS ZENITH.

AT the beginning of the 14th century Northampton was at the very height of its prosperity. Never before, and never since, has it occupied such a position among the towns of England as it then held.

After the completion of the conquest of Wales, the importance of our town was illustrated in a gruesome, but none the less in a very significant way. When David of Wales had been executed for treason, his body was cut into four quarters, one being sent to each of the leading English towns, while the head was exhibited in London. Northampton received one of these ghastly relics, the other three being sent to York, Winchester, and Bristol.

A few years later came the expulsion of the Jews: Ever since the riots of Richard I.'s time, the popular feeling against this unhappy race had continually grown more intense. All sorts of charges were brought against them, more and more restrictions were imposed upon their actions. In 1277, over two hundred of them were hanged at Northampton for clipping the coinage. That same year it was alleged that a Christian child had been enticed into the Jewry and there crucified. True or false, the tale was believed, and numerous executions followed.

To-day, if you go into the churchyard of St. Sepulchre's, you will find, built into the wall of a house standing south-east of the church, a curious stone carving representing a crucified figure, the lower part of the body being draped. There is a popular, though absurd, tradition to the effect that this carving was wrought in memory of the supposed crime! There can, however, be little doubt that it is really an ordinary churchyard or gable cross.

In 1290 the Jews were all driven out of England. Edward I. had found a substitute for them in the Lombard bankers who, though Christians, had no scruples in lending money for interest. Many of these Italians came to Northampton, carrying on their business in the empty houses in Gold Street and Silver Street. So for the first time the national arms of Lombardy were hung outside the shops of the money-lenders in our town, and Northampton burgesses in search of a loan learnt to make their way to the houses that displayed the sign of the three gilt balls.

Such loans at this time were probably sought mainly by those who were desirous of extending their business, not by people in financial straits, for the trade of our town was now increasing rapidly. In spite of the havoc wrought by civil strife during the barons' wars in preceding reigns, the number of houses was growing so fast that the burgesses were beginning to consider the question of extending the walls. In 1301 this change was brought about. The extension was made on the eastern side of the town, the new wall going south-east from the North Gate along the lines of Campbell Street and the Upper and Lower Mounts, thence following the course of York Road, Cheyne Walk, and Cattle Market Road. The new East Gate was just west of the modern Bradlaugh statue, a postern gate was built at what is now the lower end of York Road, while the new Water Gate, called Derngate as before, was at the corner of Cheyne Walk, Becket's Well being just outside.

By this extension St. Giles' Church was included within the circle of the walls. Hereafter this building plays a considerable part in the town's history, for from this time it became customary to hold the general assembly of the burgesses either in the churchyard or in the nave of the church itself. We have already noticed that to the mediæval mind there was nothing strange in the use of a consecrated building for such purposes. No doubt this particular church was selected for the meeting place of the townsmen because it was remote from the Castle and from St. Andrew's Priory, there thus being less likelihood of observation or interference by the two authorities whose wishes sometimes clashed with those of the citizens.

The Chequers, where the assembly had perhaps been held before, had now become the principal square of the town. Here stood the Market Cross, here stood the pillory, and here was erected the new town hall, which the burgesses built at the time of the extension of the walls. This building stood at the corner of Abington Street and Wood Hill, a site occupied by the town hall until about 1860. Gradually the Marehold and the streets surrounding it lost their importance, while the thoroughfares near the Chequers became the business quarter of the town.

We now hear for the first time of the New Drapery, a block of buildings standing on the eastern side of the street that we call the Drapery to-day. The houses on the western side, between the New Drapery and the Chequers, were then called the Glovery. The block we call Mercers Row seems to have been the site of some houses as early as the reign of Richard I., when it was called Wimplers Row. In the time of Edward I., it was sometimes spoken of as the Old Drapery.

Ever since 1295, Simon de Montfort's plan of having important boroughs represented in Parliament by two burgesses had been regularly practised. Northampton was represented by two of its leading citizens in the first Model Parliament of that year, and thereafter our town has always sent two members to the House of Commons. During the reign of Edward II., Parliament was twice summoned to meet in our town, just as the old Great Council had been in earlier times.

The prominent position Northampton occupied at this date is shown by the fact that it sent a larger contingent of men to the Scottish war than any other town in England except Winchester. After the murder of Edward II., Mortimer and Queen Isabella, who were ruling the country in the name of the boy king, Edward III., resolved to abandon all hope of conquering Scotland. They therefore summoned a Parliament to meet here in 1328, in order to discuss terms of peace. By the Treaty of Northampton, which was drawn up and signed at the Castle, England formally acknowledged Scotland's independence.

This treaty, which was naturally very unpopular, was one of the chief causes of Mortimer's fall. Two years later, Edward asserted the right to rule the country himself; Mortimer was executed and Isabella confined to Castle Rising for life. An ample sum was set apart from the royal revenue to provide for her wants. Part of her income was derived from the £120 *firma*, which Northampton still paid, and which Edward III. assigned to his mother for her lifetime.

About this time a case was tried before the travelling justices at Northampton, which shows us how the town managed to pay the *firma*, and which also reveals the extraordinary extent of the power exercised by the municipal authorities of this period.

Northampton was then traversed by two main highways, which ran through the town, one from north to south, and one from east to west. Along these roads passed a great number of merchants, pilgrims, and travellers of all sorts. So many were they, that near the South and West Bridges two hermits lived, who subsisted solely upon the alms given them by wayfarers who desired to be remembered in the prayers of these holy men.

Had these alms been the only expenses incidental to passing through the town, travellers would have had nothing of which to complain. Northampton, however, like all other towns possessing a royal charter, made strangers pay a heavy toll for the privilege of passing through the gates.

The obvious way out of the difficulty from the point of view of the travelling merchant, was to avoid passing through Northampton, by making a slight detour. Our ancestors, however, foresaw this possibility and provided against it by having toll stations at various outlying points on the roads around the town, *e.g.*, at Billing Bridge. It was hardly worth anyone's while to go far enough out of his way to avoid all these toll-bars, especially in the days when robbers haunted the less frequented roads.

So far the Northampton bailiffs were quite within their rights. Of course, if the inhabitants of a town possessing similar privileges were made to pay the toll, they would retaliate upon the next Northampton merchant who came into their district. Still, on the whole, our forefathers found this toll-gathering a most profitable undertaking, and they accordingly resolved to extend the scope of their operations, At the beginning of Edward III.'s reign they had the audacity to start a new toll-station at Slipton, a little village nearly twenty miles from Northampton. Here they levied toll upon everyone who passed, even upon those going from one village in the neighbourhood to another.

This was going a little too far, in more senses than one. Complaints were made, and finally the matter came before the travelling justices. At the trial numerous burgesses appeared and solemnly affirmed that they had taken toll at Slipton ever since the time of Henry III ! The jury decided against them, and it was ordered that, in future, toll should only be taken from those who went round by Slipton to escape passing through Northampton.

This Slipton incident is not one that redounds to the credit of the town, but it shows the power and importance of Northampton during this period. Not many towns were strong enough to enforce the payment of illegal dues, even for a time, at a point nearly twenty miles from their walls.

Indeed, at this time, many people must have thought it probable that Northampton, with its enlarged boundaries, its rapidly increasing municipal privileges, and its reputation as a parliamentary centre and a royal residence, would soon be second to no town in England. Such was not to be its destiny ; Northampton's prosperity had already reached its highest point, and the centuries that followed were fated to witness its decline.

CHAPTER XVI.

THE DECLINE OF NORTHAMPTON.

WE have traced the growth of Northampton from the time when it was a small Anglo-Saxon village by the riverside to the days when it ranked among the greatest of the English boroughs. Now we have before us the less pleasant duty of recording its decline from the lofty position it had attained under the three Edwards, of watching it slowly diminish in size and importance until at last it is nothing more than an obscure market town. Not until the 19th century, when the development of the boot and shoe industry again brought Northampton into fame, did our town regain anything approaching the prominence that it once possessed.

You will remember the reasons that caused the rapid rise of Northampton after the Norman Conquest. The king then needed a central stronghold, from which he could strike swiftly at any turbulent barons, to which he could summon his Great Council, and which was within a reasonable distance of the Welsh border, the Scottish border, London, and the ports from which he could reach Normandy. Northampton's geographical situation made it suitable for such a purpose, while Simon de Senlis' energy and ability made the town a place fit to become a royal residence. The royal presence led to royal favour, royal favour gained the town its charter, and the charter brought flourishing trade and increased prosperity.

Now let us consider how conditions had changed by the middle of the 14th century. After the great feudal revolt of 1174, the baronage no longer aimed at local independence. Wales was conquered by 1284; no serious attempt was made to bring Scotland under the English rule after 1328, the work of repelling and of avenging frontier raids being left to powerful border lords like the Percies. In 1337, the Hundred Years War began, and thereafter the attention of the king was centred upon the conquest of France. The earlier kings had been occupied to some extent with continental affairs, but they had never attempted to assert a claim to the French throne, and, moreover, they had generally to consider the possibility of rebellion at home. Edward III. was quite free from this danger, and consequently he and his successors did not spend much time at an inland town like Northampton. Parliament was generally summoned to London, which was within easy reach of the continent.

Of course, to a tyrant such as John, whose last years were spent in trying to crush the national resistance aroused by his evil acts, a fortress like Northampton Castle was of considerable value. After his death the repair of its fortifications seems to have been neglected, for, in Henry III.'s time, Peter de Montfort and Ralph Basset only held it against the royal forces for a single day, once the enemy had got into the town. Edward I. did not need an inland fortress in the midlands, and so took no steps to restore the Castle. Edward II., at a time when he had had trouble with the baronage, and was anticipating further disturbances, sent two officials to find out in what condition the Castle was. Their report was most unfavourable; they said that the Great Hall had been destroyed by fire three years previously, that the fortifications were in a state of decay, that several of the towers had been broken down, and that the barbican needed rebuilding. To restore the whole to a state of efficiency, they estimated, would cost well over £1,000. After this, no serious attempt was made to rebuild the fortifications. Another hall was erected, and the Castle was made fit for habitation, but hereafter it was more of a gaol than a fortress.

The last Parliament that met in the Castle was that of 1338, which was summoned to vote supplies for the French war. Edward III. did not attend; he was engaged in Flanders, so the Black Prince, a child of eight, nominally presided over this meeting, which only lasted ten days.

Edward III. held a tournament here in 1342, at which one knight was killed and many others badly wounded. This was the last visit that he made to the town.

Seven years later came the terrible Black Death. No exact calculation was ever made as to the number of people that perished during this awful time, but it is estimated at something between one-third and one-half of the entire population. We do not know how many died at Northampton, but at least six, and perhaps seven, of the nine incumbents of the town churches fell victims to the plague. The Abbess of De La Pré and the Master of St. John's Hospital are amongst those whose deaths are recorded. What the death rate among the ordinary population of the town was, we can only guess.

There is no reason to suppose that Northampton suffered more severely from the Black Death than the rest of England, but our town had fewer opportunities of recovering from the effects of its ravages than some. At this time the greatest English industry was the exportation of wool to Flanders. This business was centred in the "staple" towns, all situated near the sea coast; these places had a monopoly of the wool export trade conferred upon them by the king. In earlier times the "staple" town had been on the continent, and all English traders had had an equal chance of taking wool thither and selling it. Now it had to be exported from one of the English "staple" towns. We have seen how our own burgesses handicapped strangers who traded in Northampton. It was the same elsewhere, so we can realise that Northampton's profits from the wool trade were not great.

Thus, at the very time when our town was ceasing to be a royal residence and a meeting-place for Parliaments, it was prevented by its geographical position from becoming a great trading centre. The burgesses who extended the walls in 1301 were providing for the future growth of a town that was not destined to increase in size for many a long year. Much of the new ground enclosed by the extension was not built upon till the middle of the 19th century.

In 1380, the advisers of the boy king, Richard II., summoned to Northampton the last Parliament that ever met in this town. It was held here because a certain man had to be tried before it for murdering the Genoese ambassador. Much sympathy with the accused was felt by the citizens of London, and, if he had been condemned and executed there, a dangerous riot would probably have taken place.

This Parliament assembled in a large room at St. Andrew's Priory, because by now the Castle was in a very ruinous condition. For the same reason, the young king took up his temporary abode at Moulton.

Parliament was opened by Richard in person, and then his chancellor, Simon de Sudbury, Archbishop of Canterbury, asked the Commons to make a grant of £160,000 to the king. After debating the matter they replied that this was too much, but that they would grant £100,000, if the clergy agreed to supply a third of the amount. The spokesman of the Commons argued that they ought to do so, as they owned at least a third of the land. The representatives of the clergy were at first very indignant at this suggestion, but, after holding a special meeting in All Saints' Church to discuss the matter, they finally agreed to accept the proposal.

The money granted was raised by a poll-tax, which pressed very heavily upon the poor of the country. This was one of the causes of the Peasants' Revolt of the following year, in the course of which the rebels captured the Chancellor and cut off his head. Northampton was not altogether unaffected by the revolutionary spirit, as we hear of one William Napton exciting the poorer people of the town against the rich merchants.

The hostile feeling towards the Church, which is reflected in Chaucer's works, may also be noticed in the attitude of the Commons over the question of the £100,000 grant. There was a general impression abroad that many of the clergy spent their lives in ease and idleness, and that the friars in particular had deteriorated greatly since the days when they first came to England. The Lollard movement encouraged this feeling against the clergy. Northampton, being no great distance from Lutterworth, was considerably influenced by the doctrines of Wycliffe. A written complaint to the king by an opponent of the Lollards, one Richard Stormesworth, wool merchant, of Northampton, throws some light on the condition of things in this town.

In this complaint, Richard Stormesworth said that the mayor, John Fox, was a Lollard, and had influenced the burgesses in their favour to such an extent that the whole town was tainted with Lollardy. John Fox kept Lollard preachers at his house, and was friendly with another Lollard, who was living as a kind of paying guest at St. Andrew's Priory " where he hath caused such debate between ye Prior and Monkes that ye house is well nigh undone." One day, John Fox brought " an Herretick " to preach in All Saints' Church. On another occasion he brought in the parson of Wynkpole, a notorious Lollard, and, when the vicar of All Saints' went to the altar to sing mass, the mayor ran out and caught hold of the back of his vestment, to make him stop, because he wanted his Wynkpole friend to preach. The vicar refused to stop, and so the Lollard had to wait till the afternoon, when he got up into the pulpit to address the congregation. Richard Stormesworth promptly interrupted the sermon and told the preacher to hold his peace and come down. On this a tremendous uproar ensued, and Richard feared for his life. The mayor afterwards had Richard convicted before his court for causing a disturbance ; hence this complaint.

Richard II. unlike his Northampton namesake, was inclined to favour the Lollards, so probably this complaint was without effect. Under Henry IV. and Henry V., the Lollards were sternly suppressed. Neither of these kings came to Northampton, and no important events took place here during their reigns. Indeed, from this time onward, Northampton plays a much less important part in our national history. On the other hand, the records of local events now become more detailed, and, although our town is no longer the seat of kings and the centre of Parliamentary activity, its municipal life continues to flourish. From time to time, moreover, it chances that some great scene in the drama of England's history takes place near our town. Such was the case in 1460, when Northampton gave its name to the battle which is described in our next chapter.

CHAPTER XVII.

THE BATTLE OF NORTHAMPTON.

THE Wars of the Roses consisted of a series of campaigns in which powerful nobles, each aided by his band of retainers, fought against one another for purely selfish reasons, the struggle becoming very embittered in its later stages owing to the blood feuds that sprang into existence between the opposing families The majority of the nation took no part in the wars, rightly regarding them as mere fraction fights in which no great principle was involved. Hence we do not find the Northampton burgesses siding actively with either party, although in all probability they favoured the Yorkists rather than the Lancastrians. The leaders of the former party were no less cruel, ambitious, and selfish than their opponents, but they were at any rate capable of maintaining order in the kingdom, while Henry VI. and the corrupt clique of nobles that surrounded him were not.

In a war in which the leaders are actuated by no principles of any kind, it is not strange to find treachery rampant among the subordinate commanders Thus it was that in 1459, when the rival armies were facing one another near Ludlow, one of the chief mercenary captains suddenly deserted the Yorkists and went over to the Lancastrians. The result was a panic among the supporters of the White Rose, the Yorkist army melted away, and its leaders fled from the country.

The Lancastrians, elated by the confusion that had fallen upon their foes, called a Parliament together at Coventry and caused bills of attainder to be passed against the fugitive Yorkist chiefs. Their triumph was short-lived. The Earl of Salisbury and his son the Earl of Warwick, afterwards known as the Kingmaker, had taken refuge in Calais, together with young Edward, Earl of March, who was destined in later days to rule England as Edward IV. These three at once began to prepare for another struggle. In June, 1460, they landed in the south of England with a band of veterans from the Calais garrison.

This invasion took the Lancastrians by surprise. Their forces were dispersed, and, before most of their leaders knew that the Yorkists had landed, the invading force had reached London, which threw open its gates to them. Leaving Salisbury to besiege the Tower, which was held for Henry VI. by a few of his followers, Warwick and Edward rapidly marched northward to attack the king's supporters at Coventry.

Henry himself, a mild-tempered, religious man, was quite incapable of coping with the situation, but the old Duke of Buckingham, who was with him at Coventry, at once took charge of affairs. Sending the queen and her infant son away to a place of safety, he gathered together such troops as he could muster, and marched to Northampton in order to check the Yorkist advance.

It was nearly two hundred years since our town had been the scene of military operations. The Castle was no longer defensible, and the town walls were falling into a ruinous condition. Buckingham never thought of trying to defend Northampton itself, but constructed a fortified camp in the meadows that lie between De La Pré and the Nene. It is hard to understand why he selected this particular spot. The situation has no natural advantages, being over-looked by rising ground on almost every side, and having the river in its immediate rear.

Buckingham resolved to strengthen his position by every means in his power. Earthworks were erected and lined with cannon, while in front of these ramparts the Lancastrians dug a deep ditch and filled it with pointed stakes. When the fortifications were completed on all sides, Buckingham brought the king from the Franciscan Friary in Northampton, where he had been staying, and put him in a place of safety at the back of the camp. He then stationed an outpost at Hardingstone and awaited the arrival of the hostile army.

Meanwhile the Yorkists were advancing northward, gathering their supporters around them as they went. On July 9th their army was reported to be approaching Blisworth from Towcester. When the next morning dawned, their host was seen to be drawn up upon the slopes of Hunsbury Hill.

During the morning of July 10th, an attempt was made to settle matters by negotiation. Amid a heavy downpour of rain, the Bishop of Salisbury was seen to be approaching the Lancastrian encampment under a flag of truce. Buckingham asked what brought him there; he replied that Warwick had sent him to ask for an interview with the king. This request was met by a blunt refusal, as was also a suggestion that the quarrel should be referred to the arbitration of the Archbishop of Canterbury and the papal legate Coppini. Heralds and messengers went backward and forward between the two camps for several hours, but no result came from these negotiations. Nothing now remained but the arbitrament of war.

The rain had altered the military position of affairs in two ways. Firstly, the gunpowder of the Lancastrians was soaked through and through, so that their cannon were now of little avail. In those days, however, cannon were not very serviceable at the best of times; cold steel was still the decisive factor in battle. Secondly, the rain had converted the low-lying meadows into a veritable quagmire and had partly filled the Lancastrian trenches with water.

To some extent this second result outweighed the first, as the camp was now protected by a natural moat, so it was not without some confidence that Buckingham made his final dispositions for the impending battle. He put each of the nobles who commanded under him in charge of a particular section of the rampart, the defence of the left flank being entrusted to Lord Grey of Ruthyn, a noble from the Welsh border.

It was about two o'clock when the Yorkist army advanced. A sudden rush overwhelmed the Hardingstone outpost, and then Warwick, already an experienced soldier, although still quite a young man, prepared for the attack upon the main position. First of all, he ordered his men to give no quarter to the Lancastrian nobles and knights, but to be careful not to injure the king, and to spare any common soldiers who surrendered. Then the trumpets sounded the advance, and, in three divisions, the Yorkist men-at-arms, hampered by their heavy plate armour, moved slowly down the London Road towards the river. Edward, who was barely twenty, led the vanguard. It was his first battle, he was taking his first lesson in warcraft from the powerful baron under whom he served, a lesson from which he profited, as Warwick found out to his cost some ten years afterwards at Barnet.

As the attackers approached within bowshot, arrows from the ramparts began to whizz through the air. The Yorkist bowmen, who were advancing on the flank of the men-at-arms, returned shot for shot. Already one or two men on either side lay gasping out their lives upon the ground, when the attacking columns left the road and, bearing to the right, moved across the swampy water-meadows. Breaking into a clumsy run, the Yorkist men-at-arms splashed heavily through the mud, making directly for the Lancastrian entrenchments.

But here their difficulties began; strive as they would, not a man could obtain a footing on the slippery clay bank that confronted them. With savage shouts of triumph the defenders thrust at the staggering men-at-arms, driving them back into the water with which the ditch was filled. Again and again the attack surged on; again and again it was repelled. In vain did Warwick urge on his men with cries of encouragement, in vain did he himself lead the assault. The slope of the earthwork ran red with Yorkist blood.

Suddenly, above the terrible din of the fray, there arose from the camp a loud cry of "Treason!" A man-at arms stood on the top of the rampart waving a flag on which was displayed the Ragged Staff of the Nevilles. He was not one of Warwick's retainers, but wore the surcoat of Lord Grey of Ruthyn. That baron had turned traitor, and already his men were helping the attackers up the rampart.

Buckingham made a last desperate effort to rally his followers, but it was of no avail. Like a relentless torrent, the Yorkists poured into the camp, and on every side the defenders were falling back before the triumphant onset fo their foes. Some surrendered, some fought to the bitter end, some tried to escape and were drowned while attempting to cross the swollen river. Buckingham, when he saw that all was lost, took his stand before the royal tent, and there died as a soldier should.

Poor Henry VI. does not seem to have made any attempt to fly, but surrendered himself to the victors without a struggle. The Archbishop of Canterbury and the Bishop of London, who had watched the fight from the hill on which Eleanor's Cross stands, now came to the king and led him to De La Pré Abbey. In the grounds of that convent the bodies of many of the slain were buried. After Henry had recovered from the shock that the battle must have caused to his gentle, kindly soul, he was brought into Northampton "wythe processyone" by the triumphant Yorkists. Here, "he rested hym III. dayes and thanne came to London." Buckingham's corpse was taken by the Grey Friars and buried in their church.

We need not trace the further vicissitudes of the Wars of the Roses in these pages. It concerns us more closely that it was near Northampton that Edward IV. contracted the marriage that caused his quarrel with Warwick. While hunting in Whittlebury Forest, which lies to the south of Towcester, he was met by Elizabeth Woodville, the beautiful widow of a Lancastrian knight who had fallen in battle. She sought him with the sole intention of beseeching him to annul the act of attainder that had been passed against her late husband. The young king instantly fell in love with her, and shortly afterwards they were secretly married in the Manor House at Grafton Regis.

Warwick was angered by this marriage, more especially because Edward bestowed many favours upon the queen's Lancastrian relatives. The powerful baron consequently raised a rebellion against the king, although he himself did not take the field. The royal forces were defeated at Edgecote, near Banbury, and their leader, the Earl of Pembroke, was brought a prisoner to Northampton, and beheaded in the market square by the rebels. Edward himself was captured by Warwick at Olney, and for a time was forced to submit to the wishes of the Kingmaker. In the end, however, Warwick was defeated and slain at Barnet.

The Wars of the Roses did not affect Northampton greatly, except in so far as they led to the breaking up of the old mediæval system and the establishment of the despotism of the Tudors. We shall see in the next two chapters how our town fared under the new dynasty.

CHAPTER XVIII.

TIMES OF CHANGE.

AT the end of the 15th century, the old order of things was passing. The mediæval Church was losing its hold over the minds of men, and the beginning of the Reformation was at hand. The system of villeinage was breaking up; the power of the great barons was at an end; the mail-clad knight was disappearing from the battle-field. Everywhere the darkness of the Middle Ages was fading away before the dawn of the Renaissance.

In our own town, too, the spirit of change was in the air, The early days of the reign of Henry VII. witnessed a complete alteration of the system of municipal government. It will be remembered that it had been the custom for the mayor to be elected by the general assembly of the burgesses, who were wont to meet yearly in St. Giles' Churchyard, or in the church itself, for this purpose. Thus every citizen had some voice in the selection of those who were to govern the town. Some of the wealthier burgesses now desired to keep all power in their own hands, and presented a petition to the king, asking him to intervene on their behalf. In 1489, a special Act of Parliament was passed to meet the case. By this Act, which describes the majority of the burgesses as being "of lytell substance and haveour, and of no sadness, discrecion, wisdome, nor reason," it was decreed that the general assembly should no longer have any share in the government of the town. All power was placed in the hands of the mayor, the bailiffs, those who had been mayor or bailiff in the past, and a body of forty-eight men selected by the above-mentioned persons. This little clique was to choose the town officials in the future and was also to nominate fresh persons to fill any vacancies caused by death among the forty-eight.

Thus, exactly three hundred years after Northampton gained its first charter, the majority of the inhabitants of the town were robbed of their civic rights. Henceforth all municipal power was in the hands of a small body of rich men. This state of things lasted until 1835, and, until about 1660, it was by the votes of these few privileged individuals that the two members of Parliament were elected. Not only were ordinary citizens deprived of all power of electing their own representatives, but even the right of criticising the actions of the town officials was taken from them. One of the first steps taken by the new rulers of the town was to make it a penal offence for anyone to use "royotous and maliciouse" language against the mayor or against his advisers. As the mayor and his council decided what language was, or was not, "royotous and maliciouse," this new regulation was, in effect, a prohibition of all criticism of the new municipal authorities.

Possibly the real author of the act that wrought this change was the notorious Richard Empson. This man, who began life as the son of a poor sieve-maker of Towcester, gained the favour of Henry VII., and the hatred of a good many other people, by the skill that he displayed in extorting money from rich men to fill the royal coffers. As Empson was one of the members of Parliament for Northamptonshire, and recorder of our town, Henry's views of affairs in this part of the country would naturally be influenced to a great extent by what his favourite told him. When Henry VIII. succeeded his father, the new king made a bid for popularity by having Empson arrested on a preposterous charge of treason. The fallen minister was tried and condemned at Northampton, his execution taking place in London, on Tower Hill.

Empson was not guilty of treason, or of anything approaching treason, but if he was really responsible for the act that deprived Northampton of self-government, his tragic end was only what he deserved. Had his object been deliberately to bring the town to ruin, he could not have chosen a better way to accomplish his aim. The general assembly had not always been wise or far-seeing in its action; its meetings had frequently been characterised by violence; some of the regulations sanctioned by it had been neither just nor expedient.

But the fact that every citizen had possessed a voice in the government of the town had stimulated a feeling of public spirit, had prevented any gross injustice to burgesses, and had made each man feel that his private interests must give way to the general good of the community. When the control of municipal power was taken from the general public and given to a close corporation, it was not strange that Northampton's prosperity decayed more rapidly than ever, until at length it was little more than a small market borough, with nothing but the mouldering remains of a disused Castle, and the ruins of walls that lay far beyond the actual limits of the town, to remind its inhabitants of its former glories.

In its diminished state the town was beginning to find difficulty in raising the *firma* of £120 which had to be paid every year to the king. Edward IV. and Richard III. had both granted temporary remissions of a portion of the amount. Finally, in 1514, Henry VIII. permanently reduced the *firma* to £98, and gave up all claim to arrears from past years which were still owing. This king was not in the habit of voluntarily renouncing money due to him, except in very urgent cases, so it may be judged from his action that Northampton's decline had been very marked indeed.

Frequent signs of the forlorn condition of our town meet us in this reign. In 1533, Leland, the king's librarian, who made a tour through England to inspect the towns and villages in his royal master's dominions, noted that all the old houses in Northampton were built of stone, but the new ones of wood. Coupled with the Act of Parliament, passed two years later, this tells a sad tale of the desolation existing here at this period.

In 1535, an act was passed by Parliament to remedy the condition of Northampton and certain other inland towns. It stated that Northampton was then, and had for a long time been, in great ruin and decay, and that many empty spaces existed, covered only with the remains of dilapidated houses. To improve this evil state of affairs, it was ordered that, unless the owners of these ruined houses rebuilt them within three years, the ground landlord might do so, and then the houses would be his absolutely. If the ground landlord failed to do this, the municipal authorities were entitled to do so. If they too failed, anybody who chose to rebuild the houses might take possession of them and of the ground upon which they stood.

This act marks the lowest ebb of Northampton's prosperity. It is not known exactly what effect it had; it certainly did not raise the town to anything like its old level. From now until the beginning of the 19th century, Northampton never aspired to be anything more than the county town of the shire, but we do not hear of any further falling off. It was no longer a place that kings would choose as their residence, it was no longer familiar to statesmen as the frequent scene of important councils and Parliaments, it was no longer a vigorous self-governing community, actively striving to promote its own trade and to handicap that of strangers. But, viewed simply as a county town of no particular fame, it gradually acquired a certain humble prosperity and local importance of a sort. If it was not the resort of mighty kings and powerful barons, it was at any rate the market town to which the neighbouring farmers and gentry came to make their weekly purchases. The old Castle was not now an important military fortress, but it was at all events the county gaol and the meeting place of the Assize Court.

Moreover, it was just at this period that Northampton began to be known as a place where one could buy a good pair of shoes. We must not over-estimate the extent of the boot and shoe industry in the town at this time; we must free our minds of any conception of Northampton then being a place that exported shoes to all parts of the world, or even to all parts of England. If you had told a Northampton cobbler of Henry VIII.'s time that, about three and a half centuries later, the skins of cattle from South America would be brought to his town as leather, there made into boots, and thence exported to be sold in Constantinople, he would have thought that you had taken leave of your senses.

Of course, in mediæval times boots and shoes had been made here, as had almost everything else. King John's household accounts show that he bought a pair of dress boots here for the sum of one shilling, and also that he expended sixpence in the purchase of a pair of slippers. This does not show that our town was then especially noted for such goods: the king happened to require footwear at a time when he chanced to be in Northampton, so he bought it in the town, as he would have bought it under similar circumstances at Oxford or Canterbury. Every town, and almost every village, then made its own boots and shoes. No machinery was used in their manufacture at that time, and hence they were just as easily made in one place as in another. Even if one town had excelled in this particular industry, any attempt to sell such wares in another town, except at fair time, would have been promptly crushed by the jealousy of the local shoemakers.

Hence in the Middle Ages no particular town had been noted for boot-making. But in this matter, too, the spirit of change was working. The old prejudice against strangers and the policy of handicapping their trade died hard, but at last it was beginning to die. Slowly, very slowly, the idea was gaining ground that, if the inhabitants of one town were particularly skilled in making one article, and the inhabitants of another skilled in making a different article, it was to the advantage of both, if each specialised in the industry in which each excelled and then sold its goods to the other.

So Northampton, deprived of any large share in the wool trade by its geographical position, began to specialise more and more in the manufacture of boots and shoes. We cannot say exactly when this movement began, indeed nothing could be more difficult than to determine the exact year in which our town first contained a larger percentage of cobblers than did the average town. It is not till about 1640, that we have any record of large orders from outside the town, not until the coming of machinery was it possible for the boot and shoe trade to grow to such dimensions as to make Northampton's name known throughout the civilised world. But by the end of the Tudor period it was a common saying in England that " You know when you are within a mile of Northampton by the smell of the leather and the noise of the lapstones."

CHAPTER XIX.

THE REFORMATION.

IN 1535, whenever Northampton burgesses, who chanced to meet in street, market-place, or tavern, began to talk over current events, their conversation must have centred chiefly around two topics. Firstly, they would have speculated as to whether the new act of that year was likely to restore the prosperity of the town to any extent, and secondly, they would have exchanged a word or two about the recent breach between Henry VIII. and the pope, and its probable effect upon the religious houses in this locality.

In truth, the storm of destruction that was so soon to descend upon the English monasteries was lowering ominously at this time. Henry VIII. had already decided that they were to be dissolved, but, in order to give some colour of justice to the great robbery planned by the king and his unscrupulous minister, Thomas Cromwell, commissioners were first sent round to investigate the conditions prevailing in the religious houses in this country. These royal envoys knew well what was expected of them, and in the majority of cases their reports were most unfavourable. The official reports of the commissioners are no longer extant, but many letters written by the agents of Cromwell to their master still exist, and these serve to throw some light upon the condition of the Northampton religious houses. It must not be forgotten that the writers of these letters were strongly biassed against the monasteries, but, if they are to be believed, it seems that the once powerful Priory of St. Andrew had shared in the general decline of the town. One of Cromwell's agents writes to his master as follows :—

" At St. Andrew's, in Northampton, the house is in debt greatly, the lands sold and mortgaged, the farms let out, and the rent received beforehand." He goes on to suggest that if the king would take the Priory into his hands, this bad state of things might be remedied.

Henry VIII. had already every intention of taking it into his hands, and in 1538 he did so. By the end of that year every religious house in Northampton had been dissolved. The White Friars, the Black Friars, the Grey Friars, and the Austin Friars were all driven from their abodes, as were also the Canons of St. James' Abbey, a religious house situated on the further side of the West Bridge. To this day, the name of St. James' End recalls its existence to us, but nothing is left of the original monastic buildings, save a fragment of the precinct wall. The name of De La Pré Abbey remains, but none of the old fabric is to be found in the present house.

The treatment of the nuns of De La Pré seems to have been particularly unjust. In 1536, the aged Abbess, hoping to secure perfect safety for the convent under her charge, paid the king a large sum for a charter, in which Henry granted to her and to the nuns the privilege of holding their possessions of him for ever. None the less, in two years' time she was compelled to surrender her house. The forlorn plight of the unhappy woman, thus turned adrift into a world of which she knew nothing, moved even the stony hearts of the royal officials. One of these interceded for her, saying that for over thirty years she had ruled her convent well, that she was now old and infirm, and that it would not cost much to provide her with an annual pension, as she could not possibly live very long. Eventually the Abbess was allowed a pension of £40 a year, but the other nuns were not so well treated, the highest annual pension given to any one of them being £2 13s. 4d. The Abbey property was managed for a time by the royal officials and was then granted to a rich Londoner, in exchange for some property that he owned elsewhere. In later years the estate passed through various hands, until, about a hundred and fifty years ago, it was sold to the Bouverie family, who possess it still.

It was during the 16th century that Northamptonshire became a county that contained the residence of many wealthy families. In earlier times the town had not been greatly influenced by the county, partly because very few barons cared to live quite so near a well-known royal resort, and partly because the town had once been too powerful and wealthy to tolerate much interference from outside persons. Henry VIII. hoped, by a judicious distribution of the plunder obtained from the monasteries, to bring into existence a new class of wealthy land-owners, dependent upon the crown, and opposed to the Church of Rome, from the robbery of which their riches had been derived. Many members of this new aristocracy took up their abode in Northamptonshire, and in later years their descendants exercised all the influence usually possessed by county magnates over a small market town.

Among those who became landed proprietors at this time was a Northampton burgess named Lawrence Washington. This Lawrence Washington, a direct ancestor of the great founder of the American Republic, acquired the manor of Sulgrave from the confiscated estates of St. Andrew's Priory. Lawrence Washington seems to have been a prominent man in Northampton; he was twice elected mayor, and his name also appears among those of the first trustees of the Free School founded by Thomas Chipsey.

We know very few details of the life of Thomas Chipsey, grocer, of Northampton. He seems to have been a man in comfortable circumstances, and he was certainly one who made good use of his wealth. In 1541, three years after the dissolution of the greater monasteries, he founded and endowed a grammar school for the education of the boys of his native town. To Lawrence Washington and nineteen other trustees he made over certain lands that he possessed in Holcot, Coton, and Pitsford, on condition that they employed a master to teach "grammar" (a term then used to describe learning of any kind) without charge to any boys of the town who desired to learn. The master was to receive £9 per annum for his services, 10s. a year was to be paid to every boy selected to sing at mass in All Saints' Church, and any money that remained over was to be devoted to the repair of the market-place.

Such was the small beginning to which we owe the existence of the present Northampton School. The Free School, as it was called in early times, was at first held in a small house known as the Sign of the Lamb, which was situated in Bridge Street. This building then belonged to the Gild of St. Mary.

This gild was not one of the merchant gilds of which we have spoken in an earlier chapter. These had mostly ceased to exist by this time, and in all towns of importance their place had been taken by a number of craft gilds, each of which was an association comprising all those concerned in some particular trade or handicraft. Besides these, there were the religious gilds, to which class belonged the Gild of St. Mary.

When we speak of religious gilds, we must not forget that the other classes of gilds had to some extent a religious character. Their main purpose, however, was the regulation of trade, while gilds such as that of St. Mary existed principally for charitable and religious ends. These religious gilds, of which there were many in Northampton, generally took their name from some well-known saint, or some holy shrine. One of the most famous of those in this town was the Fraternity of the Rood in the Wall, a gild named after a crucifix built into the wall of St. Gregory's Church. We do not know the date of the foundation of this Church, but it was probably erected in Norman times. It stood in a street situated a little to the east of St. Peter's. The origin of the stone crucifix is unknown, so is its ultimate fate, but it certainly was greatly revered at one time. Henry VIII. himself made an offering at this shrine, when he was staying at Pipewell Abbey in 1511, some time before his breach with Rome. Nearly thirty years later, he stayed a night in the town, while on his way to York,

Although he had quarrelled with the pope, Henry VIII. remained a Catholic to the end of his life, but at his death the reforming party in the Church gained the ascendancy. Then came the downfall of the religious gilds. Their wealth made them a desirable prey in the eyes of the greedy councillors who ruled for Edward VI.; their Catholic origin made them obnoxious to the reforming party. The Fraternity of the Rood in the Wall shared the fate of the rest; the sacred emblem from which it derived its name was probably destroyed. There is no evidence to connect the crucifix now near St. Sepulchre's with the one that our ancestors once honoured in St. Gregory's.

The craft gilds did not escape the hand of the spoiler; much of the money devoted by them to religious purposes was confiscated. But associations similar to the craft gilds continued to exist, indeed, it is just after the dissolution of the religious gilds that we find the mayor and corporation engaged in making regulations about the Craft of the Shoemakers. As these rules not only give an idea of the nature of the craft gilds, but also show how the industry that was to make Northampton famous in later days was then growing, an abstract of them is given below.

It was ordered that every year, upon St. Crispin's Day, the master shoemakers of the town should assemble together and elect two wardens from among their number to regulate their trade. These wardens were to examine all leather that was to be offered for sale in the town. If it was of sufficiently good quality they were to stamp it; anyone who attempted to sell unstamped leather was to be fined. No shoemaker might induce a workman to leave the employ of another shoemaker by an offer of higher wages. Shoes were not to be exposed for sale in the street in front of shops, or in the market-place. No stranger was to sell shoes in the town upon pain of a fine. If anyone wished to start a shoemaker's shop in the town, he had to pay certain dues; 3s. 4d. if a native; 6s. 8d. if apprenticed here but born elsewhere; 30s. if both born and apprenticed elsewhere. The wardens were liable to be punished by the Mayor if they failed to execute their duties; part of the fines and dues they collected went to the town, part to the Craft.

It will be seen that already the boot and shoe industry was becoming important in Northampton. At the same time, the regulations illustrate the survival of the old prejudice against strangers and show why it was a long time before many Northampton boots and shoes were sold elsewhere. Just as our ancestors handicapped strangers from other towns, so did the men in other towns handicap travelling Northampton traders.

During the reign of Mary, we again hear of the Free School, In 1556, a petition was sent to Cardinal Pole by some of the principal Northampton citizens, in which it was stated that some years previously Thomas Chipsey had provided the endowment for a grammar school, but that as yet no suitable building had been obtained in which the school might be held. St. Gregory's Church, said the petitioners, was now in a ruinous condition, and no services had been held there for some years. They therefore asked that the church building should be given to the town to be converted into a school house.

Cardinal Pole granted this request, and for over three hundred years the Free School stood on the site formerly occupied by St. Gregory's Church. There are probably still some among us who received their education in this building. The lane in which it stood is still called Free School Street.

There is no need to recount here the details of the terrible persecutions that darkened the later years of Mary's unhappy reign. Northampton was the scene of only one martyrdom. In August, 1557, John Kurde, a Syresham shoemaker, was brought from the dungeons of the old Castle to All Saints' Church, there to be tried for denying the doctrine of transsubstantiation. Condemned to death by the chancellor of the Bishop of Peterborough, he was taken back to his old cell to await execution. A month later they led him forth to his doom. Slowly the sad procession passed through the streets that led to the North Gate, John Rote, the vicar of St. Giles', walking beside the prisoner and endeavouring to persuade him to recant. They went through the gate, and there before them, in the stone pit just without the walls, stood the terrible stake with the faggots ready piled around it. The priest made one last effort to shake the constancy of the heroic shoemaker. "Repent, fellow, and save your life!" he cried. "If you recant your heresy, I can obtain your pardon."

John Kurde, thus offered the choice between life and

death, did not hesitate. "I have my pardon by Jesus Christ," he replied, and with these words he turned from the priest and went bravely to his fate.

John Kurde and his fellow martyrs did not die in vain. Prior to the reign of Mary there can be no doubt that the bulk of the nation were Catholic at heart. Since then, there can be no doubt that they have been Protestant.

Let us pass from those terrible times to the brighter days of Queen Elizabeth. Her settlement of the religious question was accepted by most people, among others by John Rote. But then this reverend gentleman was by no means hard to please. We first hear of him as a Roman Catholic monk in St. Andrew's Priory, he was an English Catholic when appointed to the living of St. Giles', a moderate Protestant under the rule of the Protector Somerset, and an extreme Protestant under the rule of Warwick. We have seen him a Roman Catholic again under Mary, and afterwards he accepted the Elizabethan settlement and kept his benefice until 1576, having anticipated the celebrated Vicar of Bray by over a century.

Had John Rote lived another twelve years he would no doubt have meditated the possibility of having to make a sixth change of faith, for in 1588 many men dreaded lest Philip of Spain should succeed in conquering England. But the Spanish menace passed for ever amid the thunder of the guns off Gravelines, and England's peril was over.

All over the country rejoicing burst forth. The Northampton burgesses were not behindhand in their celebration of the event. Headed by the leading townsmen, they organized a marvellous sham fight in honour of the occasion. A hall facing the Market Square was supposed to be a fort, a tower was erected on the top of it, and palisades were constructed in front of the building. One party of citizens defended this position, another attacked it. The performance lasted three days. On the first two days, the assailants were repelled, on the third day, they stormed the position and finally set the tower on fire. "This business," says one account "was well performed; and all the towns, far and near, came to see it."

Elizabeth passed through our town several times during her reign, on each occasion being officially welcomed by the municipal authorities. By the end of her reign Northampton had definitely become a thriving little market borough, no longer one of the leading towns in England, no longer a decaying, shrinking place, but simply a small county town, beginning to get a reputation for shoemaking, yet still mainly dependent upon the patronage of the surrounding land owners, and upon the purchases made by local farmers and peasants on market-days. This was a quiet and not unhappy epoch in our town's history, but only too soon was the rude blast of war to break upon the peaceful calm of Northampton.

CHAPTER XX.

THE CIVIL WAR.

"IF princes command anything which subjects may not perform, because it is against the laws of God or Nature, or impossible, yet such subjects are bound to undergo punishment without either resistance or railing or reviling, and so yield a passive obedience when they cannot yield an active one."

Thus argued the worthy Dr. Sibthorpe, vicar of Brackley, in a sermon preached by him at All Saints' Church one Sunday in the early years of Charles I.'s reign. This sermon gained for its author a royal chaplaincy and the living of Burton Latimer, for it strongly upheld the doctrines of Divine Right and Passive Obedience, that were so dear to the Stuart kings. But it may well be doubted whether the reverend gentleman's discourse was equally appreciated by the congregation that listened to it, for Northampton had the reputation of being one of the most Puritan towns in England, and its inhabitants were bitterly opposed to the pretensions of Charles I.

Ever since Elizabethan times our town and the district around it had been a centre of the Puritan movement. Robert Browne, the founder of the Independents, spent the greater part of his life here and finally died in the Castle Gaol, his body being interred in St. Giles' Churchyard. At Fawsley Hall, one of the celebrated Martin Marprelate Tracts was printed. These writings were directed against the established Church, and, whatever may have been their faults, no one can complain that their style lacked vigour. They alluded to the Archbishop of Canterbury as "the Canterbury Caiaphas," to the bishops as "incarnate devils," and to the clergy in general as "dolts, hogs, drunkards, foxes, dogs, desperate and forlorn atheists." The hand of the law fell heavily upon those responsible for the production of these abusive tracts.

John Penry, their author, was hanged, and Sir Richard Knightley, the owner of Fawsley Hall, was fined £2,000 for allowing one of them to be printed in his house.

This incident took place towards the end of Elizabeth's reign. Throughout the reign of James I., Puritanism continued to increase in this locality. Northampton received Charles I. and Henrietta Maria with every outward appearance of loyalty when they passed through the town in 1634, but the vigorous protest made by the Corporation two years later against the ship-money tax shows that the king's attempt to make himself absolute was warmly resented here.

Naturally Archbishop Laud's endeavours to enforce a more careful observance of religious ceremony in church services were very unpopular in our Puritan town. Thomas Ball, the vicar of All Saints', was a whole-hearted Puritan himself, and a letter of complaint, sent by one of his parishioners to Laud, shows us that the vicar had the support of most of his congregation.

The author of this letter, one Mr. Ramsdell, says that he himself does his best to follow the archbishop's injunctions, and that thus he has incurred considerable unpopularity. After enumerating the various ways in which Laud's commands have been disobeyed at All Saints', and saying that Mr. Rogers, the Headmaster of the Free School, is an open Nonconformist, and never comes to church, he continues as follows :—

"I am smiled at by the ministers and better sort, and laughed out of church by the vulgar. The men are a little more sparing herein than heretofore, but the women and boys never so forward, which makes me think they set them on. A tradesman's maid watching me bow my head said 'Take heed of your nose, for I hear of one that lately did fall down and bruise his face as he was bowing!' And a tradesman's son did run a stool against me foot foremost when I did obeisance. I am counted a papist, they say, throughout the town. There cannot be a more scornful parish and people in England."

Thomas Ball was continually in trouble with the authorities. In May, 1640, he was brought up before the Star Chamber. A few months later he refused to pray for the king's success against the Scots in the Second Bishops' War, and would no doubt have been punished had not the king been forced to call the Long Parliament, which imprisoned Laud and thus saved the Puritan vicar.

As the crisis in the relations between king and Parliament daily drew nearer, signs were not wanting that Northampton would take the side of the latter if war broke out. Early in 1641, the corporation began to prepare the town for defence against a possible attack and to consider the question of repairing the ruined walls. It was ordered that the stones of a disused church should be utilised to build up the breaches, and that the gates should be repaired and strengthened. All the burgesses who had muskets were to provide themselves with powder and bullets; twenty men were to be on guard nightly in each of the four wards into which the town was then divided.

In 1642, the Great Civil War began. Northampton was selected as the rendezvous for the Parliamentary army that was to be placed under the command of the Earl of Essex. Troops began to pour into the town from all sides during the early part of September.

We possess an excellent account of those days in the letters written to a London friend by one Nehemiah Wharton, a Puritan sergeant in a company of musketeers. They serve to show us how different the Parliamentary levies were in every way from the splendid army that Cromwell brought into being during the later years of the war.

On September 1st, a considerable Roundhead force set out from Coventry to march to Northampton, Nehemiah Wharton and his musketeers being among them. On the first day they got no further than Long Buckby, where they had considerable difficulty in finding shelter for the night. The village church was crowded with tired soldiers, while some of the less fortunate "were glad to dispossess the very swine." Nehemiah slept in no pig-sty; with foresight that would have done credit to a veteran campaigner, he mounted one of his soldiers on a horse and sent him on ahead of the main body to arrange for accommodation for his officer.

Next morning, in spite of the fact that Holdenby House was garrisoned by five hundred Royalist musketeers, who were on the look-out for stragglers, the men seemed to have wandered all over the countryside searching for plunder. One of them came back arrayed in a surplice, hood, and cap that he had stolen from some priest's house, and announced that he was the Archbishop of Canterbury. This delicate touch of humour seems to have tickled our friend Nehemiah greatly.

At length the march was resumed, although the officers appear to have had some difficulty in restraining their men whenever they passed a house that seemed to offer prospects of loot. The army arrived at Northampton towards evening and settled down for the night. The Earl of Northampton, head of the famous Compton family, was a staunch supporter of the king, and boldly rode into the town to spy out the strength of the Roundhead forces. His presence was discovered in the morning, but he managed to get away in safety.

Nehemiah and his fellow-soldiers spent nearly a fortnight in Northampton. They appear to have divided their time about equally between listening to sermons and making expeditions into the country in search of plunder. Monday, September 4th, was a most eventful day for Nehemiah. In the morning he took twenty of his men out to " search the house " of a certain " base priest " who lived six miles away, However, the " base priest " escaped the threatened visitation. for, when the party had gone about two miles, they received news that some of the army were engaged in plundering a house close at hand. Dividing his men into three sections, Nehemiah surrounded the plunderers and, according to his own account, made them return what they had taken. He goes on to say that out of sheer gratitude the owner of the house presented him with a fine scarlet coat lined with plush and several books of his own choosing. Possibly the presence of the twenty musketeers had something to do with this generosity. Nehemiah, congratulating himself upon a good day's work, turned back towards Northampton. He had not gone very far before his little force was stopped by a troop of Roundhead horse, also in search of booty. They took Nehemiah's newly acquired possessions from him and even robbed him of his sword. Indignant at this insult, he swore that he would order his men to fire unless the weapon were restored to him. The horseman returned it and then made off, leaving Nehemiah to make his way back to Northampton, "threatening revenge upon the base troopers." His company then drew lots as to which of them should watch the South Gate, so as to be able to regain the lost possessions of the sergeant. As the freebooting horsemen straggled in by twos and threes during Monday night and Tuesday, Nehemiah searched them carefully, but, although he took from them a "fat buck and a venison pasty," he failed to recover his scarlet coat and books.

Nehemiah's next trouble was a mutiny in his company. When marched out to drill on Thursday morning, they declined to obey orders unless they received five shillings a head first. John Hampden and other officers came out and harangued them, apparently without much effect.

Next morning, Nehemiah's company was paraded to hear a lengthy sermon from a Puritan divine, one Obadiah Sedgewick. Another sermon was arranged for the afternoon, but the musketeers were spared this, as news came that Prince Rupert was plundering Market Harborough, and the army was mustered to meet a possible attack. Next morning, the postponed sermon was preached, and in the afternoon the army marched out to welcome Essex, who entered the town with much pomp. On Saturday night and Sunday, Nehemiah's company was on duty guarding the North Gate. They thus escaped two further sermons. On Wednesday, a great review was held, and in the evening the whole army marched away in the direction of Rugby.

We must now take leave of our friend Nehemiah Wharton, as he marches through the North Gate and out of sight with his musketeers, and must consider the war as it affected our district. The work of restoring the wall continued steadily and, under the command of Colonel Whetham, the garrison daily grew more and more efficient. Constant skirmishing went on all over the county, but not until a year later did an engagement of any importance take place near this town.

One Saturday evening, in October, 1643, the news came that Rupert's horsemen had been seen in Long Buckby. At once all was stir and excitement, the walls were lined with musketeers, and a force of cavalry rode out to Kingsthorpe to await the enemy. Thence an advanced party was dispatched to Brampton Bridge to scout. Ere long they came galloping back along the road, bearing the news that they had come into touch with Rupert's advanced guard, one of whom they had slain, while a Roundhead trooper had been wounded in the arm. Hardly had this report been given, when the clatter of horses' hoofs announced the approach of the enemy. The Roundheads fell back before the determined onset of their foes and rode rapidly away in the direction of the town, with Rupert's Cavaliers hard at their heels.

It was a clear moonlight night, and the musketeers who lined the wall near the North Gate soon realised the situation. As the pursuing force, closely following upon the track of the retreating cavalry, arrived within musket range, a heavy volley greeted them. The Cavaliers, seeing that to advance further would be to court annihilation, reined in their horses and awaited the arrival of their infantry. The North Gate was then opened, and the Parliamentarian cavalry rode through into safety.

Ere long, the Royalist infantry came up, but they were not in sufficient strength to attempt an assault, while the Roundheads were unable to harm the enemy's cavalry by musketry fire, as they had ridden out of range. A desultory exchange of shots took place between the Royalist musketeers and the defenders of the wall, but the former never came very close, so little damage was done to either side. Finally, the Roundhead cannon were brought into action, a round shot from the town tearing its way through the ranks of the opposing cavalry and killing two men. At this the Royalists began to move off, and ere long the Northampton garrison had the satisfaction of seeing the last of them disappear into Kingsthorpe Hollow. Thence they made their way by Moulton Park to Billing Bridge, where they crossed the Nene and went on into Bedfordshire.

When morning dawned, the Roundhead cavalry again went out of the North Gate to hunt for stragglers. These are always plentiful after an engagement at night; on this occasion not less than forty were captured.

Space does not permit a detailed account of the numerous skirmishes that took place in this district during the next two years. In December, 1643, a detachment of the Northampton garrison, under the command of Colonel Whetham, assisted Major-general Skippon in an attack upon Grafton House, which was held by the Royalists. The house was surrendered on Christmas Eve.

Early next year, a body of Roundhead infantry, about forty strong, marched out of our town to forage in the neighbourhood of Canon's Ashby. During the night they were surprised by a superior force of Cavaliers and were forced to take refuge in a village church, where they resisted desperately.

At length the church door was blown down by a petard, and the majority of the defenders surrendered, though some still held out in the steeple. It was not until the Cavaliers prepared to burn down the steeple that this last remnant yielded to superior numbers and laid down their arms. The Roundhead prisoners were taken off to Banbury, but their captivity was not of long duration, for, about a week later, Colonel Whetham arrived at Banbury with a large force and effected a rescue.

In June, 1644, one of the main Royalist armies, under Charles I. himself, was at Brackley operating against the Parliamentarian force commanded by General Waller. The latter was beaten at Cropredy Bridge on June 29th, and a few days later his defeated army arrived at Northampton. We can imagine the scene when the vanquished troops, some seven thousand of them in all, marched wearily through the South Gate into the town. We can picture to ourselves the feelings of the citizens and their wives as they scanned the ranks of the war-stained, foot-sore soldiers, some wounded, all tired and dispirited, looking in vain for the face of some friend or relative who had been slain in the recent battle.

Next year the Northampton garrison sent out about 400 men to levy contributions in the neighbourhood of Daventry. Here they were attacked by a force under the command of two of the Comptons, who were supported by Sir Marmaduke Langdale with a body of Royalist cavalry. The Roundheads retired in some confusion from the enemy, who had a marked superiority in numbers. The Cavaliers pressed them closely, killing 13 and capturing no less than 36.

On March 18th, about three weeks after the event recorded above, a cavalry skirmish took place near Kingsthorpe between the Northampton garrison and the Earl of Northampton's Cavaliers. The accounts given of this affray are very conflicting, but the Royalists again appear to have obtained the advantage.

Yet, though there were a few minor Royalist successes in this neighbourhood, the king's cause was already doomed. The battle of Marston Moor had established the supremacy of Parliament in the north, and ere long another equally crushing defeat in the midlands was to rob Charles of all hope of ultimate triumph. As this final blow was struck within a few miles of Northampton, we shall endeavour to trace the details of the eventful battle of Naseby in our next chapter.

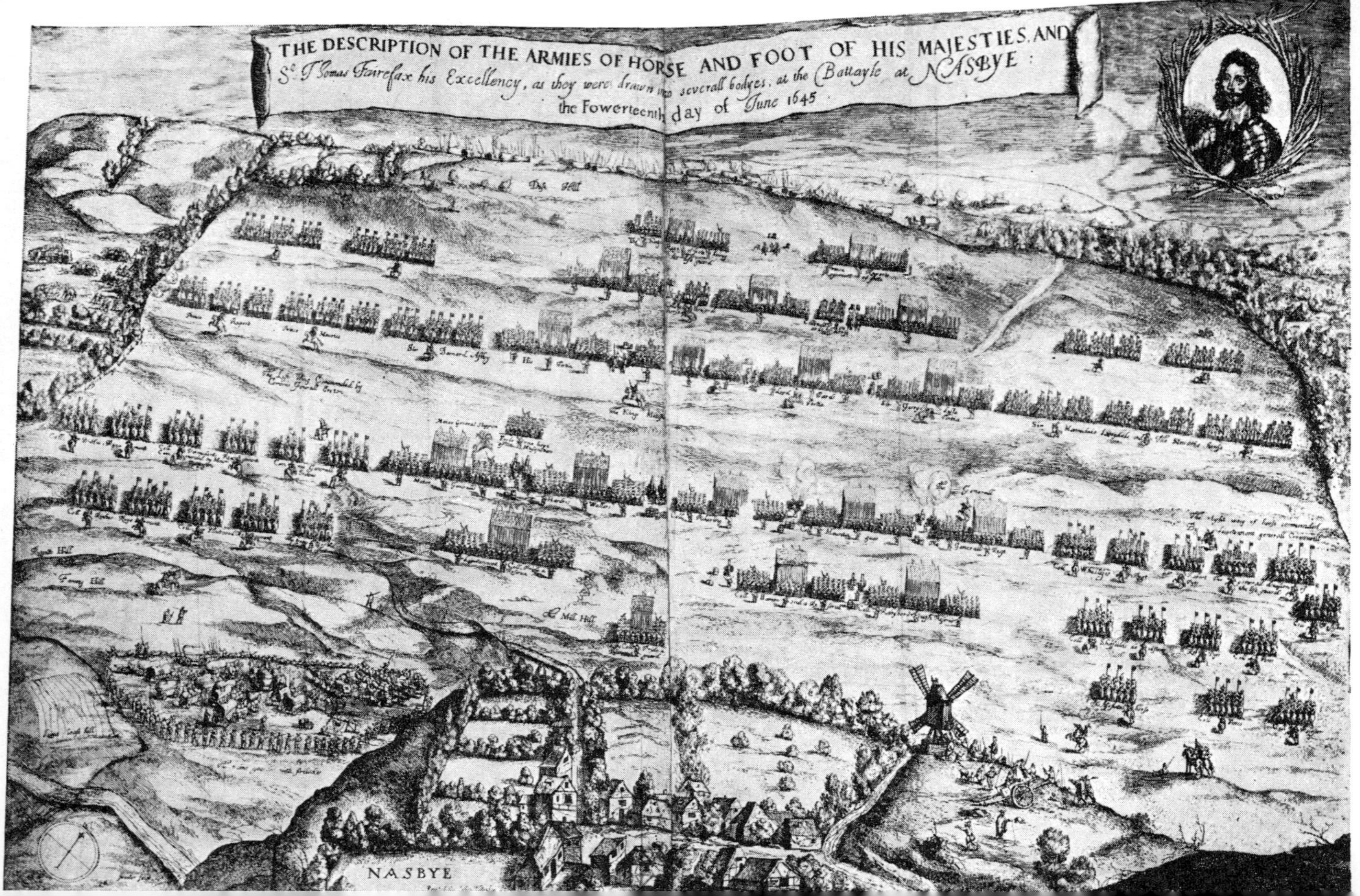
THE DESCRIPTION OF THE ARMIES OF HORSE AND FOOT OF HIS MAJESTIES, AND
Sr. Thomas Fairefax his Excellency, as they were drawn into severall bodyes, at the Battayle at NASBYE:
the Fowerteenth day of June 1645
Mill Hill
NASBYE

CHAPTER XXI.

NASEBY FIGHT.

TO follow in detail the movements of Charles I.'s army, from the time he left Oxford in 1645, until the day that his troops first came into touch with the New Model, would be as futile as it would be tedious. The king had no definite object in view, at one time he was thinking of making his way north to join hands with Montrose, at another he contemplated an attack upon the Eastern Association, while some of his commanders hoped that he would move into the west to aid Goring. Meanwhile, news came to him that Sir Thomas Fairfax was besieging Oxford, and so, after the royal army had taken Leicester, Charles resolved to abandon his more ambitious plans until he had relieved his threatened headquarters and had provisioned Oxford sufficiently to enable him to leave that city without being burdened by the continual fear that it would be surrounded and starved into submission during his absence.

Thus it was that, on June 7th, the Royal army marched into Daventry and thence to Borough Hill, where an encampment was formed. No sooner had they arrived there than a message came that the siege of Oxford had been raised. It was therefore no longer necessary to march back to relieve that city, but Charles determined that, before he went away, he would collect cattle and provisions from the country round and send them there. So for nearly a week the Royalists remained at Daventry, their troopers foraging in the neighbouring villages and thus gradually collecting supplies together. They had no idea that the enemy's main army was anywhere in the vicinity.

Such, however, was in fact the case. Fairfax had abandoned the siege of Oxford on June 5th, and since that date he had been steadily approaching the Royalist army, to which he intended to give battle. On the 11th he arrived at Wootton, where he was met by the Mayor of Northampton, who, aided by the townspeople, endeavoured to supply the army with such necessities and comforts as could be provided. Next day the army went on to Kislingbury, and, before evening, Fairfax's scouts had been sighted by the Royalist sentinels on Borough Hill.

So little was Charles prepared for news of the immediate proximity of the Roundheads that, when he first heard of their approach, he was engaged in hunting a stag in Fawsley Park. At once all outlying bodies of troops were called in, and the whole army encamped for the night on Borough Hill. Charles now resolved to retire in the direction of Leicester and accordingly moved off to the north before daybreak. As early as three o'clock in the morning, Fairfax himself, who had spent the night in riding round his outposts, observed the flames of burning huts on the hill-side, which enlightened him as to the enemy's intention. By five o'clock, the Roundhead scouts had come in with the intelligence that the whole Royalist army was retreating in the direction of Market Harborough.

An hour later, Fairfax called a council of war. As the stern-faced, soberly-clad Puritan commanders sat in their general's tent discussing what should be done, a sudden burst of cheering from the camp without reached their ears. A moment later a shout of, "Ironsides!" "Ironsides has come to lead us!" told them its cause. Oliver Cromwell himself, at the head of 600 cavalry, had just ridden into Kislingbury. He had come on ahead of the main body of his troops in order to be present at the battle which he realised was now imminent.

Encouraged by the presence of the great commander, the council of war at once determined to follow up the retiring enemy with all speed. Ireton was sent on in front with a picked body of horsemen to harass the retreat of the Cavaliers.

Meanwhile the Royalist army was making its way towards Market Harborough. The main body arrived there unmolested towards sunset, but some of the cavalry detached to cover the rearguard fell into a trap through over-confidence.

In seeming forgetfulness of the proximity of the enemy, they halted at Naseby, through which their army had just passed, and settled down to eat their supper in a house in the village. Such behaviour seems little short of madness, and it brought the result one might have expected. A body of Ireton's horse rode into the village, surprised the revellers at their cups, and captured them to a man.

Such was the news that Charles received as he was about to seek his bed in the little village of Lubenham. He immediately went into Harborough and aroused Prince Rupert, who had already gone to bed, to discuss the situation with him and the other commanders. It was plain that if the retreat was continued, their rear would be in perpetual danger from the Roundhead cavalry. Finally, it was resolved to stay and offer battle the next day.

Early next morning the Royalist trumpets sounded the advance, and the whole army moved out of Market Harborough to a ridge near Sibbertoft, about a mile to the south of the town. Here the 7,500 men who composed the Cavalier force were drawn up in order of battle. On the right were about 2,000 horsemen under the command of Rupert, on the left about 1,600 more under Sir Marmaduke Langdale, while in reserve were about 500 picked cavalry and some of the best infantry, under the king himself. The main body of the foot were placed in the centre under the veteran Astley.

The first intention was to stand fast and await the attack of the enemy, and, had this plan been adhered to, the issue of the battle might have been different. But, as hour after hour passed without any sign of the enemy being seen, Rupert's fiery spirit began to chafe under the delay. At last, after scouts had been sent out and had come back saying that they could see nothing of the Roundheads, the Prince himself took a party forward to investigate matters. Charles watched him and his men disappear in the direction of Clipston, wondering what had happened to the enemy. He did not have long to wait. Ere many minutes had passed a messenger came riding back in hot haste from Rupert. He bore a statement that the whole Roundhead force was in retreat, and that the Cavaliers must move forward at once. Thereupon, the king's army abandoned its excellent position and advanced, not without some confusion, in the direction of Naseby village.

To understand how it was that Rupert came to send back such a report, we must return for a moment to the Roundhead force, whom we left pursuing the retreating Cavaliers on the morning of the 13th. On the evening of that day, the main body of Fairfax's army halted at Guilsborough, though, as we have seen, Ireton's cavalry pushed on as far as Naseby, where they captured some of the Royalist rearguard.

Early on the morning of the 14th, the Parliamentarian army advanced northward, and by five o'clock they were at Naseby village. North of this the ground is very undulating. Just outside the village there is a slight depression, then the ground rises to Mill Hill, which is about a mile from the church. From Mill Hill northward is a gentle descent to what is called Broadmoor. Then again the ground rises to Dust Hill, the summit of which is about a mile from the top of Mill Hill. The numerous hedges that now intersect Broadmoor did not exist in the seventeenth century. One, however, was there even at that time, the double fence interspersed with thickets of bramble, which is known as Sulby Hedge.

When the Roundhead army arrived at Naseby, Fairfax was informed by spies that the enemy were in the neighbourhood of Market Harborough. He accordingly drew up his men in battle array along the crest of Mill Hill, Cromwell being in command of the cavalry wing on the right, Ireton on the left, Major-general Skippon and Fairfax himself commanding the infantry in the centre. The Parliamentarians thus stood ready either to defend the position they held, or to advance and attack the enemy.

Cromwell's quick eye, however, soon detected that the Roundheads were not taking full advantage of the ground. There was no need to wait on the actual crest of the hill, where their numbers and dispositions could be seen, when by going back about a hundred paces they could remain in concealment and at the same time could easily advance to the crest again if necessary. At his suggestion the whole force was moved back a little. It was this movement that Rupert had observed, and from it he had formed his erroneous conclusion that the Parliamentarians were retreating.

Thus, hardly had the new position been taken up, than the Roundheads, looking over the top of Dust Hill, saw the king's army, horse, foot, and guns, pouring over Sibbertoft Ridge into the valley that lay between them and Dust Hill. The Cavaliers were evidently about to attack.

In spite of the marked superiority in the foot-soldiers that Fairfax possessed, it must have been with some anxiety that he watched the approach of the Royalists. The rank and file of the New Model were many of them raw recruits, whose courage had yet to be tested, while the hostile army was composed of war-hardened veterans. But, Cromwell, confident of the justice of his cause, felt nothing but exultation at the thought of the impending conflict. Some months after the battle he writes :—

" I will say this of Naseby, that when I saw the enemy draw up and march in gallant order towards us, and we a company of poor, ignorant men to seek how to order our battle, I could not, riding alone about my business, but smile out to God in praises, in assurance of victory, because God would, by things that are not, bring to naught things that are, of which I had great assurance—and God did it."

For a while the advancing Royalists were hidden from sight by Dust Hill. Skippon meantime detached a body of dragoons under Colonel Okey to line Sulby Hedge, whence, having dismounted, they could pour in a heavy volley upon the Royalist right wing as it advanced. A body of three hundred musketeers was sent down the hill in front of the Roundhead centre, with orders to retire on the main body if they were hard pressed.

Ere long, the leading files of the Royalists appeared upon the crest of Dust Hill. With loud shouts of " Queen Mary ! " they advanced rapidly down the slope towards the Roundhead position, amid the thunder of Fairfax's cannon. The advanced party of musketeers fell back, firing as they went, and in a few minutes the battle had joined all along the line.

On the Royalist right, Rupert carried all before him. Okey's dragoons fired volley after volley, but could not check the wild charge of the prince's cavalry. Like a whirlwind the mass of horsemen swept up the hill, driving Ireton's troopers back in confusion. The Roundheads did not move forward together, some regiments charged and some hung back, with the result that their left wing was completely shattered. Ireton himself, who had allowed his attention to be diverted to the infantry struggle on his right, had his horse shot under him. Wounded in the face with a halbert and pierced through the thigh with a pike, he was forced to surrender. Elated at their success, the victorious Cavaliers chased their opponents right into Naseby village, slashing and thrusting at the flying Roundhead troopers. They even attacked the Parliamentary baggage train, but were met by a volley from the musketeers who guarded it.

Meanwhile in the centre a stubborn fight was raging. Outnumbered as they were, the Cavaliers pressed on with much resolution, and here, too, their soldiers were forcing the Roundheads back. Skippon was wounded in the side, but he gallantly refused to leave the field. Fairfax's regiment of foot stood their ground, but the rest of the infantry were driven back on the reserves.

So on the Royalist right and centre all was going well. It was quite otherwise on their left. Here Sir Marmaduke Langdale faced Cromwell, and, although the latter's horsemen were hampered by some furze bushes and by the unevenness of the ground, they charged down upon the Cavaliers with such vigour that they swept them back in complete disorder, only a few rallying on Rupert's reserve of foot.

Thus on either side the right wing of cavalry had beaten the force opposed to it, while in the centre the battle was still undecided, though the Royalist infantry were steadily gaining ground. So far it seemed that the day was going in the king's favour, but the whole situation was altered by the splendid discipline displayed by Cromwell's men, and by Rupert's complete lack of control over his Cavalier horsemen. As we have seen, the Royalists on the right wing were scattered all over the countryside in pursuit of the cavalry they had routed. In this part of the field the victors were as useless for military purposes as were the vanquished. It was quite otherwise with the cavalry that Cromwell commanded. No sooner had Langdale's horsemen been put to flight, than the Puritan troopers re-formed their ranks and awaited fresh orders. A few regiments were dispatched to follow up the beaten Royalists and to prevent them from rallying; the remainder wheeled to the left and fell like a thunderbolt upon the flank of the enemy's infantry.

The Royalist foot-soldiers, still occupied by their struggle with the Roundhead infantry, had no chance whatever of making an effective stand against this fresh attack. Cromwell's troopers pitilessly rode them down, while the Parliamentarian centre, encouraged by the arrival of the cavalry, rallied again and supported the efforts of the horsemen. On every side the king's foot-soldiers began to throw down their arms and to cry for quarter.

Charles, with the Royalist cavalry reserve, for a moment sat looking aghast at this sudden change of fortune. Whatever his faults may have been, the king did not lack courage. Already some of Rupert's horsemen were straggling back, and Charles himself had 500 picked cavalry, who were quite fresh. He resolved to try to retrieve the disaster that had befallen his infanty by one last desperate charge, but, even as he was about to lead his men into action, the Earl of Carnewarth seized the bridle of his charger, swerving the animal round to the right, and cried, "Sire, will you go to your death in an instant?" The king hesitated for a moment; his troops took the movement of his horse as a signal for retreat. Some unknown person shouted, "March to the right!" and, before Charles could restrain them, the whole cavalry reserve had wheeled round and ridden off the field. Rupert returned from his pursuit of the Parliamentarian left, only to find that the day was lost.

The Royalist cavalry made good their retreat to Leicester, although they were pursued almost up to the walls of that town by their victorious foes. Charles's infantry were almost all captured or slain. One regiment held out gallantly for a time, but finally a simultaneous charge in front and rear, directed by Fairfax himself, overwhelmed them. Fairfax, who had displayed the greatest possible courage throughout the day, cut down the standard-bearer of the Royalist regiment with his own hand. A trooper picked up the fallen banner and afterwards boasted that he had slain the ensign who had borne it. When Fairfax heard of the tale, he simply said: "I have honour enough; let him take that honour to himself."

The battle of Naseby was fatal to the Royalist cause. About 4,000 prisoners were taken by the victors, many of whom were lodged in the Northampton churches during the night they stayed in the town, while on their way to London. All the king's artillery fell into the hands of his foes, as did most of his baggage. Amongst other things, the Roundheads gained possession of the letters that has passed between the king and Henrietta Maria, the publication of which helped to turn the opinion of the country against Charles.

To-day, a first glance at Naseby field reveals nothing, save a monument that stands some distance from the actual battle-field, to show that this peaceful spot was once the scene of a desperate and bloody struggle. Closer investigation will, however, bring to light many traces of the fight that raged here in bygone days. Sulby Hedge still stands; some of the old trees that line it are pocked with bullet marks to this day. Deep depressions in the ground still mark the places where the bodies of the slain were buried. Even now, Naseby ploughmen occasionally find in their furrows one of the big leaden bullets used on the eventful day that marked the downfall of the cause of Charles I.

NORTHAMPTON CASTLE. (VIEW OF OLD WALL, LOOKING N. E.).
Reproduced from The Rev. R. M. SERJEANTSON's "Castle of Northampton," by permission of the Author, and the Northants. Natural History Society.

CHAPTER XXII.

THE COMMONWEALTH.

"HONEST men served you faithfully in this action. Sir, they are trusty. I beseech you in the name of God not to discourage them."

Thus wrote Oliver Cromwell from Market Harborough to the Presbyterian Speaker of the House of Commons, only a few hours after the last shot had been fired on Naseby field. The passage quoted above was cut out of his letter when Parliament published it, for the Presbyterian members had no intention of circulating Cromwell's plea for the Independents, the "honest men" who had won victory after victory for the Puritan cause.

Indeed, soon after Naseby Fight, the breach between the Presbyterian Parliament and the Independent New Model began to widen. Ere long it became obvious that no agreement could be arrived at between the two factions, and that Charles intended to take full advantage of their dissensions.

It was not until about two years later that matters actually came to a head. By this time the war was over. Charles, who had surrendered to the Scots before Newark, had been handed over to the Parliamentary Commissioners in January, 1647. They had taken him to Holdenby House, which was at that time the king's property. Here the defeated monarch remained for some months, while the dispute between Parliament and the army grew daily more bitter.

At last the army resolved to seize the king, and to make terms with him themselves, as the Parliamentary proposals to Charles involved the establishment of Presbyterianism and the persecution of the Independents. Cornet Joyce, a cavalry officer, was deputed to carry out this important mission.

On the evening of June 3rd, Cornet Joyce, at the head of a detachment of cavalry, arrived at Holdenby House and asked to see the king. The Commissioners protested that Charles was already in bed, but Joyce insisted upon seeing him, and eventually the king arose and came down to meet the Puritan officer. Joyce then apologised for disturbing Charles, but said that it was necessary to take him away lest the Parliament should do so. Having asked various questions as to the treatment he would receive at the hands of the army, Charles finally consented to go with Joyce. The soldiers appointed by Parliament to guard the royal captive were not numerous enough to offer any resistance to Joyce's force, and, at about one o'clock on June 4th, the king was taken away in the direction of Newmarket. Before his departure, he asked Joyce where was the commission by virtue of which he did this deed. The cornet pointed to the line of veteran troopers drawn up in the courtyard of the house. "There is my commission," said he bluntly. "As fair and well-written a commission as ever I have seen" replied the king laughingly; he was far from sorry to leave Holdenby.

In recounting the important events that took place in the neighbourhood of Northampton, we have been forced to neglect the town itself. It must not be imagined that the ordinary everyday life of England was suspended throughout the war. We are apt to concentrate our attention upon the principal actors in that great drama and to forget the thousands of Englishmen who went stolidly on with their usual work, what time others fought and triumphed, or fought and died, on the bloodstained fields of Marston Moor and Naseby. Just as to-day when there is a general election in progress, the result of which may be of vital importance to the country, it is only a small minority who actually take an active part in the canvassing and speech-making that go on, so in the seventeenth century only a few people took part in the battle and sieges of the Civil War.

In Northampton the bulk of the inhabitants lived their usual lives during these eventful years. The Master of the Free School was far more concerned about the amount that the trustees would allow him to pay for an usher, than about the sum the Scots would require before they would hand over the king to the Parliamentary Commissioners. The local cobblers no doubt exhibited more interest in the prospect of a big order for soldiers' boots than in the future fortunes of the wearers of their goods.

In point of fact, it is during the Civil War that we first hear of large contracts for boots being executed in this town. Boots are very important things to those engaged in warfare; an army that cannot march to the battlefield is not of much service; few men can march far or rapidly unless they are well shod. The constant hard wear involved in continual marching makes frequent renewals of an army's footwear a prime necessity to military success.

In earlier chapters we have traced from the beginning the growth of Northampton's staple industry. We have seen how our town, being excluded by geographical conditions from any great share in the wool trade, began to specialise in the manufacture of footwear in the early Tudor times. We have noticed how the jealousy of the shoemakers in other towns must have prevented any considerable export trade at first, we have also pointed out how the growth of new ideas about commerce gradually broke down the ancient prejudice against buying goods manufactured in another town. Now the Civil War produced a brisk demand for boots and shoes for the troops; we read of orders for 40,000 pairs at one time coming to Northampton. Perhaps the Parliament was naturally inclined to favour a town so widely noted for its Puritan tendencies, but, be this as it may, the fact remains that the orders came here. In the quaint words of a writer of that time, Northampton was now beginning "to stand on other men's legs."

A few months after the execution of Charles I., Northampton witnessed an attempt at rebellion on the part of the Levellers. These men were soldiers of the victorious New Model Army who, not content with the abolition of the monarchy, the House of Lords, and the Anglican Church, wished to bring about still more revolutionary changes. Their minds were full of wild ideas of universal equality and freedom from all the law. There are always a certain number of fanatical dreamers of this kind in a nation. As a rule, they are merely harmless visionaries, but visionaries trained to arms and flushed with recent victories are the reverse of harmless.

The immediate cause of the mutiny of the Levellers was the execution for insubordination of one of their leaders. Upon this, risings broke out in several parts of England. At Banbury, one Captain Thompson headed a revolt. Accompanied by about a dozen troopers, he rode into Northampton late one night, and on the following morning rode to the gaol and demanded the release of three of his friends who were imprisoned there. The gaoler was afraid to resist him, and, for two days this handful of daring fanatics seems to have overawed the whole town. They pretended that a large body of their supporters was near at hand, thus frightening the municipal authorities into submission. Thompson took possession of some arms and ammunition that were stored here, made a speech in the Market Square, announcing his intention of abolishing all taxes and tithes, and then plundered the local excise office and distributed the money he found there among the mob. His next step was to attempt to enlist recruits in the town, and it appears that several men joined him. Hearing that troops were being hurried up from Oxford to suppress the rising, he left the town and rode off in the direction of Sywell. There his little band of followers was surrounded by the pursuing soldiers, and, after a desperate resistance, Thompson, who refused all offers of quarter, was shot dead by a trooper. His body was brought back here and buried in the churchyard of All Saints'.

Perhaps the actions of extremists like Thompson turned the inhabitants of this town against the Commonwealth, for there can be no doubt that the majority of the people here welcomed the Restoration in 1660. Religious and political fanaticism were common under the Puritan rule, but both are very distasteful to the average English man. The deeds of the Quakers at this time must have caused much resentment; in 1665, we read of a woman being imprisoned for interrupting the service at one Northampton church by crying out to the minister, " Give over deceiving the people lest the judgment of the Lord fall upon thee ! " In the early days of this sect, its adherents considered it their duty to interfere actively when anything of which they did not approve was being taught. On one occasion, probably during the early days of Charles II., a Quaker made his way into the Free School, where the boys were " acting their parts in strange dresses." He protested vigorously, exhorting those in charge " to train up their children in the fear of the Lord." The Master and his usher evidently resented this intrusion, for we are told that " they did lay violently upon him with their sticks."

The rule of the Major-Generals also helped to turn public opinion against the Commonwealth. Stern, puritanical men themselves, these soldier-rulers imposed their own views upon the populace they governed, and suppressed many innocent amusements, as well as some that were by no means innocent. It had been the custom to keep bears in captivity and to bring out these unhappy animals on festive occasions to be " baited " by dogs for the amusement of the spectators. Bearward Street was so called because the residence of the official who looked after the bears was in that thoroughfare. The Major-Generals stopped bear-baiting and had the bears shot, not, it has been aptly said, because bear-baiting gave pain to the bear, but because it gave pleasure to the spectator.

One result of the Restoration was the destruction of the town walls. Charles II. had not forgotten that Northampton had been a military stronghold of the Parliamentarians during the Civil War, and he resolved that it should never play a similar part, in the event of an attempt being made to send him " on his travels again." So, early in his reign, Charles ordered the complete demolition of the walls. This work was carried out in 1662, part of the already ruined Castle being pulled down at the same time, and almost all the arms that had been gathered there being taken away.

Such was the end of Northampton's fortifications, which had existed since the time of the first Simon de Senlis. In his day they had been an urgent necessity, but after the Civil

War there was no further occasion for them. Only once again did the shadow of civil strife threaten to darken our town, and happily this proved to be a false alarm. The battles Northampton has had to fight since 1660 have been those of commercial warfare, and here our town has attained greater and more lasting renown by the assertion of its supremacy in our staple trade, than ever it did in the past upon the battle-fields of mediæval times.

CHAPTER XXIII.

THE GREAT FIRE.

TWO of the most noteworthy events in the early years of Charles II.'s reign were the Great Plague of London in 1665 and the Great Fire that took place in the following year. Neither of these closely concerns Northampton, but, by a singular coincidence, in this same reign a terrible and devastating fire occured in our own town. As for the plague, outbreaks of disease were only too common in all towns during this period. The complete neglect of modern sanitary precautions, the narrowness of ancient streets, and the amazing ignorance of the doctors of this time concerning the causes of and remedies for ill-health, led to continual severe epidemics here as elsewhere.

There was one outbreak in Northampton in Elizabeth's days, two more took place during the reign of James I., while the most terrible of all occurred just before the Civil War. The last time that we hear of the plague in Northampton is in 1647, when the Tower, a building that had flanked the water-gate in the days of the Norman kings, was used as a pest-house. It is described as having been some distance away from other buildings at that time, which shows us how the town had shrunk since its time of prosperity in the early Middle Ages.

After 1647, no outbreak of the plague in this town is mentioned in our local records. Our worst troubles from fire, however, were yet to come. Here again the narrowness of the streets was one of the prime causes, while the fact that many houses were built of wood must also have made it easy for conflagrations to spread. The means adopted to prevent fires were very primitive; twelve leather fire-buckets, six long poles with iron hooks, and eight ladders were maintained at the town's expense, while each parish was also supposed to provide a certain number of fire-buckets of its own. At one time these were kept in the various parish churches, but during the Commonwealth they were removed to the Town Hall, which, it will be remembered, then stood at the corner of Abington Street.

It was on the morning of September 20th, 1675, that the Great Fire of Northampton broke out. All are agreed that it began in the house of a poor woman in St. Mary's Street, but there is some difference of opinion as to precisely how it was started. The town clerk's account is that she was carrying a few live coals in a shovel from a neighbour's house to cook her dinner, when the wind blew some of them on to the thatch of her house. The vicar of All Saints' writes that she was using straw to heat some water, as fuel was dear, and that the burning straw set her chimney on fire. There is also some doubt as to the exact hour at which the fire began.

However this may be, it is an undoubted fact that, having once been started, the fire spread with dreadful rapidity. A strong west wind drove it towards the town, and, almost before the majority of the burgesses knew what had happened, the flames were blazing fiercely above the malt-houses in the Horsemarket.

All was confusion and panic. Hither and thither ran the frightened women and children, screaming in terror as the roar of the blazing timbers told how swiftly the fire was gaining ground. Men rushed from their shops and houses to get the fire-buckets from the Town Hall, hurried orders were shouted on every side, while above all the terrible din rang the bell of old All Saints', sounding now for the last time.

With the poor appliances at their disposal, some of the braver citizens made a gallant attempt to fight the flames. But all their endeavours were in vain, the water from the fire-buckets availed little against the raging flames that leapt from house to house and street to street, spreading destruction everywhere. Impeded and hindered by the terror-stricken fugitives, the little band of heroes fell back before the ever-growing conflagration. Gold Street was ablaze and the inhabitants were flying to save their lives, many of them clutching some cherished possession in their trembling hands.

It is recorded that one man escaped from the burning street holding a barrel of gunpowder under his coat as he ran!

Now the fire had reached the oil and tallow stores in College Street, and great jets of flame sprang to the sky as those inflammable materials caught alight. It was evident that the Drapery was doomed. A mob of terrified townspeople forced their way through the narrow opening that leads to the Market Square, bearing their goods to what they fondly imagined to be a place of safety. "All hands and arms were full, all busy in laying out and mislaying what they never shall see again," writes an eye-witness. Ere long, the square was piled high with goods and crowded with their frightened owners. who hoped that there at least they would be safe. Vain hope; already All Saints' Church was ablaze, and now the flames were spreading from the west side of the Drapery to the houses that enclosed the Market Square. Away to the south-east, huge tongues of flame could be seen, that told the panic-stricken beholders that the fire had reached the Tower. Indeed, by now all Derngate was on fire.

Soon the flames that wrapped the surrounding houses reached the goods that were stacked in the Market Square. One last desperate effort was made to extinguish them, and then, seeing themselves shut in by a wall of fire on almost every side, the unhappy owners abandoned their goods and sought to save their lives. The only avenue of escape left open to them was through the house of one Dr. Danvers, a building that still stands on the east side of the square. Through here the fugitives made their way to safety, for the house, which was detached from all other buildings, had so far been spared by the flames. A determined effort to preserve it ended successfully, and thus it still stands to remind us of that terrible day.

All through the afternoon and evening the fire raged furiously, and, when night fell, it still lit up the sky for many a mile round. Not till six o'clock on the following morning were the last embers extinguished. What a sad sight Northampton must have presented when the sun rose upon the smoking ruins of our town!

More than half the houses had been burnt down, eleven lives had been lost, and many thousands of pounds' worth of property had perished in the flames. All Saints' Church had been almost entirely destroyed, but the other principal churches had been preserved, while the Town Hall had sustained but little injury. St. Peter's parish had fared best of any, although the fire had started in that part of the town. The Free School had escaped destruction, as had most of the other buildings in that neighbourhood. But elsewhere was wide-spread ruin and misery. Thousands of homeless people stood bewailing the charred and blackened remains that alone were left of all their worldly possessions.

Prompt steps were taken to alleviate the disasters caused by the fire. Already the neighbouring gentry, headed by the Earl of Northampton, had flocked in to give what help they could. A subscription list was at once opened, the Earl heading it with a gift of £120. Men immediately set to work to erect temporary wooden shelters for the homeless people.

When the news of the catastrophe spread over England, money poured in from all sides to remedy the prevailing distress, and to help to rebuild the town. Many cities and towns made liberal donations for these purposes, London contributing no less than £5,000. Some of the surrounding villages also rendered such assistance as they could afford; for example, we read of a contribution of £11 1s. 10d. from Bugbrooke. In all, about £25,000 was collected. Charles II. himself gave 1,000 tons of timber from the royal forests to help to rebuild All Saints' Church, and remitted the chimney tax in our town for seven years.

Thanks to the generosity of their king and of their fellow subjects, it was not long before the inhabitants of Northampton saw rows of new houses filling the places of those that had been destroyed. In two respects, however, the Great Fire has had a lasting effect upon our town. In the first place, an enormous number of the town records were burnt, and thus we have comparatively few written particulars left of the mediæval life of Northampton during the days of the town's prosperity. Secondly, it is owing to the Great Fire that so ancient and famous a town as our own contains very few dwelling houses that date before the 18th century, the most noteworthy of these being the so called "Cromwell House" in Marefair, and Dr. Danver's house in the Market Square.

During the years in which Northampton was being rebuilt, all England was seething with excitement over the "Popish Plot," Shaftesbury, the politician who used the panic to further his own ambitious ends, intended if possible to exclude James, Duke of York, from the succession and to substitute for him the Duke of Monmouth. Even after Shaftesbury's fall, Monmouth endeavoured to increase his personal popularity by making tours through England, accompanied by a retinue of his most ardent supporters. In 1682 we find him at Northampton, when the town's accounts show an expenditure of £2 9s. "for the Duke of Monmouth's wine at the George." No doubt the Whig corporation thought the occasion justified them in spending a little public money in celebrating the duke's visit. They were seldom at a loss for some excuse to indulge in wine at the town's expense, as the accounts of their expenditure show.

After the dissolution of the Oxford Parliament in 1681, Charles found himself unable to inflict the vengeance he desired upon Shaftesbury, owing to the strength of the Whigs in London, where the arch-conspirator was acquitted by a Grand Jury composed of his supporters. At once the king resolved to break the power of the Whig corporations in London and elsewhere. In almost all towns it was found that the charters had been violated in some way that rendered them invalid. Charles thereupon insisted upon the surrender of the charters, granting new ones on terms that insured the supremacy of the Tory Party. Northampton's charter was surrendered in 1683, and in a new one, granted about a month later, the king took steps to secure the predominance of his supporters. Every member of the small oligarchy that was to control the municipal government was named by the king, and there can be no doubt that the majority of them were Tories. In addition, Charles reserved to himself and to his successors the right to remove any town official from his office. James II. made full use of the powers reserved to the crown under this charter, for, towards the end of his reign, he interfered with the municipal elections on no less than four occasions.

William III. visited our town on three occasions, being the last king to do so until His Majesty King George V. came to Northampton in 1913. William's presence in the town afforded the Corporation fresh opportunities of drinking wine at the public expense, opportunities of which they were not slow to avail themselves. It is to be feared that love of good living corrupted the morals of the town officials to some extent at this time, for one William Agutter, mayor in 1692, is praised by a contemporary writer because " he did not sell the town land for claret, as others did."

In 1711, during the mayoralty of John Agutter, presumably a relative of the virtuous gentleman mentioned above, it was resolved to commemorate the generosity displayed by Charles II. after the Great Fire of 1675, by placing a statue of that monarch above the portico of All Saints' Church. This figure was originally painted all over, for the mayor's accounts mention the expenditure of 14s. " for cullering King Charles." Two years later the grateful corporation went still further, and expended £3 in having the statue gilded. Traces of both paint and gilt still remain. The sculptor has represented the " Merry Monarch " as wearing a full-bottomed wig with a Roman toga, so the statue, while it serves to remind us of the most tragic event in the town's history, is yet not altogether without its humorous side.

From a Painting. *By G. Vials.*

ST. GILES' SQUARE, IN 1861. (*By kind permission of Mr. C. A. Markham*).

CHAPTER XXIV.

HANOVERIAN TIMES.

"HAPPY is the nation that has no history," is a saying not altogether without truth. If the same thing applies in an equal degree to towns, Northampton was indeed in a blissful state during the 18th century, for singularly few events of historical importance took place here during that period. It is not that we can complain of the lack of local records; after the Great Fire these are as full and detailed as those of any other town in England. From 1720 onward we have, besides the municipal records, the files of the *Northampton Mercury*, a journal which can boast of a longer uninterrupted issue than any other newspaper in the world. Yet, in spite of the abundant sources from which information about 18th century local events can be gathered, the period remains the most barren in our history.

It is almost as hard for us to picture Northampton, as it was then, as it is to imagine what our town was like in the Middle Ages. It seems inconceivable that, as late as 1800, Northampton was a sleepy little market borough with about 7,000 inhabitants. Such, however, was the case; hardly one of the thousands of houses that now form the north-eastern part of the town existed at this time. The Wellingborough Road, down which the tram-cars now move between the crowded pavements, was then a quiet country highway leading to the village of Abington. The sites of Queen's Park and Phippsville were then agricultural land, intersected by winding narrow lanes.

Such was Northampton in Hanoverian times. No one then thought that the unimportant little market town would one day be world-famous for its pre-eminence in the boot and shoe trade. Boot-making was, of course, the great industry of the town far earlier than the 18th century; we have already noted the large orders executed during the Civil War, but, until the introduction of machinery and the factory system, it was not possible for a town to rise to fame by its reputation for manufacturing articles which could be made as easily in one town as in another.

So our ancestors lived their uneventful lives here in the 18th century, no more anticipating the future industrial growth of the town than the Saxons of ancient Hamtune had anticipated that their little riverside village would soon become the residence of kings and the meeting-place of statesmen. Our Georgian forefathers were no doubt quite content with the town as they knew it, obscure and peaceful, with its public pump, stocks, and pillory in the Market Square. The Free School and the various Blue Coat, Green Coat and Orange Coat Schools that then existed supplied their children with such education as was considered needful in those days. Our ancestors were doubtless equally satisfied with the justice administered in the town, though to us some of the sentences seem extremely harsh. We read of two men being hanged here for robbing a person of a silk handkerchief, a knife, and 4d. !

The records of the courts of justice held in this town have their humorous as well as their tragic side. We hear of constant convictions in the mayor's court for using bad language. In 1729, one Brisoe Mortimer, gentleman, of Hanslope in the County of Buckinghamshire, was fined £4 12s. for "profanely swearing six and forty awful oaths!" Apparently a Northampton dyer stood by and counted up the profane expressions as they were used, subsequently laying information before the mayor. We are not informed what trying circumstances occasioned such a lengthy outburst on the part of the Buckinghamshire gentleman, but his action was not altogether without its advantages, as the money he had to pay was distributed among the poor of All Saints' Parish.

Perhaps Northampton was best known outside its immediate neighbourhood at this time as being the town in which annual "bills of mortality" were published by the Clerk of All Saints'. These documents were lists recording the number and causes of the deaths during the past year. Upon them were based the calculation of all the earlier insurance companies. Towards the end of the century, it became customary to append to these lists some verses on the uncertainty of human life. In 1787, the clerk, finding some difficulty in getting these supplied to his satisfaction by his fellow townsmen, went to the poet Cowper, who then resided at Weston Underwood, and requested him to compose some verses for the purpose. Cowper asked why he did not make use of the talent of one Mr. Cox, a Northampton statuary with some local reputation as a poet. "Alas! sir," replied the clerk, rather tactlessly, "I have heretofore borrowed help from him, but he is a gentleman of so much reading, that the people of our town cannot understand him!" In spite of this rather doubtful compliment to Cowper, the good-natured poet volunteered to supply the required verses. "A fig for poets who write epitaphs upon individuals. I have written one that serves two hundred persons!" says Cowper, when narrating the incident in a letter to a friend.

Northampton also gained some repute during the early part of the century as the residence of the celebrated Dr. Doddridge, Nonconformist preacher, teacher, and author. His friend, John Wesley, visited our town on several occasions.

It was upon one of these visits that the great founder of Methodism discovered his Northampton friend engaged in the unaccustomed work of assisting in the organization of a military force. The *Mercury*, on September 2nd, 1745, had said:—"We can assure our readers, upon authority, that our apprehension of troubles in the north-west of Scotland will ere long blow over." For once, however, the editor of this excellent journal had been misinformed. Even as he wrote, the young Pretender was marching on Edinburgh. In less than three weeks' time the royal army under Sir John Cope was beaten at Prestonpans, and England was threatened by a Jacobite invasion.

On September 26th, the principal gentlemen of the county assembled at the George Inn to decide what steps should be taken to meet so pressing a danger. It was resolved to raise and equip a volunteer force for the defence of the town. Dr. Doddridge, ever a strong supporter of the Hanoverian dynasty, took a leading part in this work.

The Volunteer force never went into action, as, after the Young Pretender's retreat from Derby, all serious danger of a Jacobite invasion passed away, but for some months continual drilling went on in the fields round Northampton. Some Jacobite sympathisers tried to dissuade men from enlisting, by circulating a rumour that those who did so would be compelled to serve in the regular army after the war. The *Mercury* for October 21st, 1745, contains a notice offering a reward of £10 for evidence leading to the conviction of any person spreading such rumours.

It will be observed how very much our town was under the influence of the nobility and gentry of the county during this period. There was nothing resembling the old mediæval spirit of municipal independence, or the vigorous civic life of the present day, in Hanoverian Northampton. The municipal officials were elected by a small oligarchy whose political views seem to have been quite alien to those of the majority of the inhabitants. It was thus by no means strange that the mass of the citizens looked for leadership in times of stress to those outside the town boundaries. Moreover, in the 18th century, when a journey to London was a long, wearisome and expensive undertaking, most of the local aristocracy did the bulk of their shopping in the county town, and upon their patronage depended to a great extent the prosperity of the Northampton tradesmen. Hence the influence exercised in our town by the county magnates was very great.

Although the municipal government was still in the hands of an oligarchy, every householder not in receipt of poor relief now had a vote in Parliamentary elections. This change appears to have taken place shortly after the Restoration. As a general rule, the candidates were the nominees of local noblemen.

The most exciting election contested in Northampton at this time took place in 1768. The Earl of Northampton and Lord Halifax "who had for many years each sent his man," this time supported Sir George Rodney and Sir George Osborne, whose candidature was also favoured by the corporation. Opposed to them was Sir James Langham, the nomineee of Earl Spencer.

It was evident from the very beginning that party feeling would run high. Early in the contest a riot ensued from the meeting of two rival processions in the streets at night. Each side mustered its supporters, and the Rodney-Osborne faction made an attack upon the George Inn, the headquarters of their opponents. A desperate struggle took place, bludgeons and stones being freely used by both sides. Next day, some hundreds of countrymen, armed with cudgels, were brought into the town as reinforcements by the Earl of Northampton and Lord Halifax. For a time matters looked very serious, but wiser counsels prevailed, and the countrymen withdrew before any further disturbance took place.

Shortly after this, Sir James Langham decided to retire from the contest "either through cowardice, or because he had been tampered with," although there was apparently a majority in his favour. Nothing daunted, Earl Spencer nominated a Mr. Thomas Howe, and the election proceeded with unabated vigour. By mutual consent, the usual oath as to bribery was not administered to voters. The poll was open for a fortnight, and every day the issue grew more uncertain. At first votes had been bought for about £10, but towards the end the price mounted to about £500.

In all, about £160,000 was spent by both sides. The declaration of the poll resulted in the following figures:—

Sir George Osborne	...	611
Sir George Rodney	...	611
Mr. Thomas Howe	...	538

The matter did not end here. Earl Spencer appealed to the House of Commons against the partiality of the mayor and his bailiffs, who had acted as the returning officers. Inquiry proved that his action was fully justified, and Mr. Howe was declared member. The other two candidates "tossed five guineas in a hat," to decide who should have the remaining seat, and Sir George Rodney won!

Such was the celebrated "spendthrift election" of 1768. The Earl of Northampton was nearly ruined by his expenses in the contest, while the failure of Sir George Osborne so preyed upon the mind of Lord Halifax that he died a year or two later.

It is a fact worthy of record that over fifteen per cent. of those who voted in this election were shoemakers. This shows that by now a considerable number of boots and shoes must have been sold every year outside the town; a much smaller percentage of shoemakers would have sufficed to supply inhabitants with footwear. Later, Northampton's increasing trade was aided by the efforts of Mr. Spencer Perceval, who was one of the borough members from 1796 until his death. As a member of the Cabinet, and afterwards as Prime Minister, he exercised his influence to secure government contracts for the bootmakers of this town. In 1812, Mr. Perceval was assassinated in the lobby of the House of Commons by a maniac named Bellingham. A monumental statue of the deceased Premier was erected in All Saints' Church; it has since been removed to the council chamber of the Guildhall.

Photo *"Northampton Independent."*

VISIT OF THEIR MAJESTIES KING GEORGE V. & QUEEN MARY TO NORTHAMPTON. SEPT. 23RD, 1913.

CHAPTER XXV.

MODERN NORTHAMPTON.

A CURIOUS feature in the history of our town is the fact that four of the most important events affecting it occurred at intervals of about three hundred years. We first hear of Northampton just after 900, its first charter was granted just before 1200, three centuries later came the act that robbed its citizens of the right of self-government, while at the beginning of the 19th century the growth of the boot and shoe trade again raised the town to a position of importance

How rapid the rise of our town has been during the past hundred years can best be judged from the study of the increase of population since the beginning of the last century. In 1801 there were about 7,000 inhabitants. Thirty years later there were 15,000; in another forty years there were over 40,000; to-day there are over 90,000.

Throughout the nineteenth century more and more houses have had to be built to shelter the growing population; far beyond the limits of the old walls the ever-increasing town has spread, until Kingsthorpe and Abington have ceased to be neighbouring villages and have become suburbs. Still the town continues to grow, and now the roads between Abington and Weston Favell are beginning to assume a suburban aspect.

This vast increase in the size and importance of a place, which only a hundred years ago was a small market borough, is due almost entirely to the effect exercised by the introduction of machinery upon the boot and shoe industry. Before the nineteenth century, when boots were all made by hand, it was as easy to manufacture them in one place as in another; to-day, when machinery of a complicated and expensive nature is employed, the natural tendency is for their manufacture to be carried on mainly in a few towns where a speciality is made of such work. This alone would not have made Northampton pre-eminent in the boot and shoe industry; we must not forget to take into account the enterprise and forethought of those manufacturers who were quick to see the advantages of the new machinery, and to make use of it. By their action they not only made fortunes for themselves and their families, but also spread far and wide the fame of their native town.

In other respects, too, Northampton has progressed greatly during the past century. The oligarchy that had controlled the municipal government since 1489 was displaced from power by the Municipal Corporations' Act, of 1835. Since then our local government has been "broad-based upon the people's will," as it was in the early days of the town's mediæval prosperity.

The general improvement in the welfare of the labouring classes all over England has nowhere been more marked than in Northampton. No town can boast of so large a proportion of workmen who own their own houses; few manufacturing centres have so low a death rate.

Education, which has made such vast strides in late years, is particularly well provided for in our town, the inhabitants of which are justly proud of the splendid elementary schools that have come into existence here since the Education Act of 1870. The Free School founded by Thomas Chipsey has progressed with the other institutions of the town. In 1867, the old building in Free School Street was abandoned, and a new school was erected in Abington Square, then on the outskirts of the town. For about forty years the Grammar School, as it was then called, remained on this spot, but in 1911, increasing numbers caused another migration, and the School now stands in the Billing Road, just outside the municipal boundary. Could Thomas Chipsey but revisit his native town and see the great mass of buildings and the spacious playing-fields that have developed from the small Free School founded by his bequest, what would not be the amazement of the worthy 16th century grocer? Yet, were he to pass the football fields, and to pause to listen to the cries that arise from them in the crisis of a "house-match," he would realise that his name was not forgotten.

Amid all the changes of the last century, it was inevitable that some of the well-known buildings of ancient times should disappear. The old Town Hall was demolished in 1864, when the first part of the new buildings in St. Giles' Square was erected. Fifteen years later the extension of the premises of the London and North-Western Railway Company involved the destruction of what remained of the Castle built by Simon de Senlis. The pillory has disappeared from the Market Square; it is now just a hundred years since it was last used.

No reigning monarch visited Northampton after William III. until 1844, when Queen Victoria passed through the town on her way to Burghley House. Edward VII. did not visit Northampton, but, as recently as 1913, His Majesty George V. was received here by the mayor and corporation.

Almost all who read this book will remember that memorable day. They will recall to their minds the crowded streets, the brightly-coloured flags, the general excitement and enthusiasm. Perhaps some were present in the Market Square and witnessed the loyal greeting accorded to His Majesty, as he ascended the dais erected for his reception.

Here, as King George stands in the central square of the town visited by so many of his predecessors, let us end the story of Northampton. We have traced the history of its past; what of its future? It lies with you, the men who must make or mar its progress hereafter. Everyone of you can do something to better your native town; on your efforts depends its destiny.

THE END.